Diary of a Wren 1940-45

Audrey Deacon, 1943.

Diary of a Wren
1940–45

by

AUDREY DEACON

The Women's Royal Navy Service, generally known as Wrens, was formed in World War I, revived at the beginning of World War II, and ceased to exist in 1993, when women became eligible to serve in the Royal Navy.

The Memoir Club

© Audrey Deacon 2001

First published in 2001 by
The Memoir Club
Whitworth Hall
Spennymoor
County Durham

British Library Cataloguing in
Publication Data.
A catalogue record for this book
is available from the
British Library.

ISBN: 1 84104 032 0

Typeset by George Wishart & Associates, Whitley Bay.
Printed by Bookcraft (Bath) Ltd.

In Memoriam
TD

Contents

1945

Illustrations

Introduction

This diary was begun in 1940, when I was twenty-two, very serious and bookish, without any view to publication during my lifetime, though I had a vague notion of making an historical record for posterity, and therefore made an effort to be accurate and objective.

I was living with my parents, Harold William and Constance Dora Hawkins (their only child), in a small house in the Milehouse district of Plymouth. My father was a headmaster in the Royal Marines. I had joined the Women's Royal Naval Service on the outbreak of war in September 1939 and was working as a Leading Wren (Writer) at the Commander in Chief's headquarters at Mount Wise, Devonport. At that time the Western Approaches Command included the South Coast of England west of the Portsmouth Command, and the West Coast extending north into Scotland. Later it was divided into the Plymouth Command and the new Western Approaches, based on Liverpool, in order to intensify the campaign against the U-boats, which at that time were causing heavy losses of shipping in the Atlantic.

I was secretary and personal assistant to the Maintenance Captain (Captain E.C. Lush), whose duties are difficult to define briefly, but might be summarized as providing liaison with many different bodies and persons on non-operational matters: at times we seemed to function almost as a naval Citizens' Advice Bureau – recipients of any type of problem. The subjects dealt with at different times included consultation with Departments of the City Council, discussions with the YMCA and Toc H, arranging for Dockyard Departments to deal with defects or difficulties in requisitioned premises, helping the newly-arrived Polish naval officers to sort out an enormous range of problems, exploring possible ways of camouflaging the china-clay spoil-heaps north of the city (which at one time were thought to be helping German bombers to pinpoint the position of Plymouth), keeping a record of the miscellaneous small vessels which arrived unannounced in Plymouth Sound from northern France during the summer of 1940, and issuing petrol coupons to naval officers who needed to use their cars for essential purposes.

After the blitzkrieg on Poland in September 1939, and the so-called 'phoney war' until April 1940, there had been, in rapid succession, the invasion of the western European countries, including France, in May and June of that year.

It was typical of the time that people took things in a very matter-of-fact way (possibly because there was no television reporting to make events larger than life, but more probably because one had to get on with the immediate tasks waiting to be done each day). It seemed reasonable to expect trains to run on time whatever happened, or to go away and leave one's house unattended during a period of frequent air-raids. Partly this was due to naiveté, I suppose, and the fact that no one really understood in advance what the effect of heavy bombing – still less invasion – would be; but on looking back, it seems quite extraordinary.

Another thing that surprised me on re-reading the diary was the impression of opulence given by the numerous week-ends in hotels. In fact the reverse was the case: pay was low, but free travel warrants were issued for seasonal leave – and of course for travel on duty – fares, hotel charges and everything else were remarkably low, and there were not many other things to spend one's money on. A bill dated December 1945 from a private hotel for two people for two nights, with meals, amounted to £3.18.9d. We usually stayed in small hotels or guest houses, occasionally in private houses: people were anxious to help members of the forces and would willingly let rooms for bed and breakfast.

The diary as written continues until 1951, but the part now presented ends in 1945. The first diary entry, for 7 September 1940 (not reproduced), was an innocuous note about having a few days' leave and the way in which I had spent my time.

The original text is unaltered except for a word or two here and there; this and added explanatory notes are indicated by square brackets. Obscure initials have been expanded to full titles; many items of current news have been cut out or condensed, but a framework of the more relevant events has been retained. Derogatory comments on individuals have been omitted, as have references to personal and private concerns of people mentioned.

In many cases it has not been possible to trace people named – or even to establish whether they are still alive. I hope, therefore, that any of them who read the diary will accept my apologies for this unavoidable omission. Many have been identified from Navy Lists of the period; but sometimes even that was difficult, e.g. if there were several people of the same surname, or, in the case of WRNS officers, who may have married after the date of the mention in the diary. I am grateful to those whom I was able to approach and who have agreed to allow their names to appear.

Special thanks are due to: three ex-WRNS friends – the late Miss Priscilla Chase MBE and Miss Ursula Thorne, who allowed me to try out the unedited text on them, and Miss Joy Hope for the Churchill photograph; Miss P. Hansell, Mrs. K. Macleod and Mrs. J. Sears for their contributions; and most of all to Dr. Doris Jones-Baker FSA, without whose encouragement and guidance the book would never have taken shape.

I have received valuable help from the Association of Wrens (Mrs. P. Wall), the Imperial War Museum (Departments of Photographs and Documents), the National Maritime Museum (the Librarians and Miss U. Stuart Mason, Head of Public Relations), the Ministry of Defence (Mr. J.D. Brown, Naval Historical Branch), the *Daily Telegraph* (Information Department), and the staff of the Public Library, St. Albans.

I am indebted to the following publishers and authors for permission to quote from the works indicated:

William Collins, Sons and Co. Ltd., for Commander K. Edwards' *Operation Neptune*

Miss U. Stuart Mason for *The Wrens 1917–77*

Underhill (Plymouth) Ltd., for H.P. Twyford's *It Came to Our Door*.

Special thanks are due to the Imperial War Museum for permission to use the photograph of Sir Winston Churchill with WRNS officers, and to The Greenwich Foundation for the Royal Naval College for the photograph of the Painted Hall.

Any profits from the sale of the book will be given to charity.

Audrey Deacon

Postscript

The various opinions expressed are, of course, those which I held at the time. Had I been writing now, with the benefit of experience and of a great deal of information which has since become available, some would be very different, perhaps especially those relating to the Nuremberg Trials (1945).

Audrey Deacon
2000

Issued by the Ministry of Information in co-operation with the War Office
and the Ministry of Home Security

Beating the INVADER

A MESSAGE FROM THE PRIME MINISTER

IF invasion comes, everyone—young or old, men and women—will be eager to play their part worthily. By far the greater part of the country will not be immediately involved. Even along our coasts, the greater part will remain unaffected. But where the enemy lands, or tries to land, there will be most violent fighting. Not only will there be the battles when the enemy tries to come ashore, but afterwards there will fall upon his lodgments very heavy British counter-attacks, and all the time the lodgments will be under the heaviest attack by British bombers. The fewer civilians or non-combatants in these areas, the better—apart from essential workers who must remain. So if you are advised by the authorities to leave the place where you live, it is your duty to go elsewhere when you are told to leave. When the attack begins, it will be too late to go ; and, unless you receive definite instructions to move, your duty then will be to stay where you are. You will have to get into the safest place you can find, and stay there until the battle is over. For all of you then the order and the duty will be : " STAND FIRM ".

This also applies to people inland if any considerable number of parachutists or air-borne troops are landed in their neighbourhood. Above all, they must not cumber the roads. Like their fellow-countrymen on the coasts, they must " STAND FIRM ". The Home Guard, supported by strong mobile columns wherever the enemy's numbers require it, will immediately come to grips with the invaders, and there is little doubt will soon destroy them.

Throughout the rest of the country where there is no fighting going on and no close cannon fire or rifle fire can be heard, everyone will govern his conduct by the second great order and duty, namely, " CARRY ON ". It may easily be some weeks before the invader has been totally destroyed, that is to say, killed or captured to the last man who has landed on our shores. Meanwhile, all work must be continued to the utmost, and no time lost.

The following notes have been prepared to tell everyone in rather more detail what to do, and they should be carefully studied. Each man and woman should think out a clear plan of personal action in accordance with the general scheme.

Winston S. Churchill

STAND FIRM

1. What do I do if fighting breaks out in my neighbourhood?

Keep indoors or in your shelter until the battle is over. If you can have a trench ready in your garden or field, so much the better. You may want to use it for protection if your house is damaged. But if you are at work, or if you have special orders, carry on as long as possible and only take cover when danger approaches. If you are on your way to work, finish your journey if you can.

If you see an enemy tank, or a few enemy soldiers, do not assume that the enemy are in control of the area. What you have seen may be a party sent on in advance, or stragglers from the main body who can easily be rounded up.

'Beating the Invader' (Government leaflet, 1941)

CARRY ON

2. What do I do in areas which are some way from the fighting?

Stay in your district and carry on. Go to work whether in shop, field, factory or office. Do your shopping, send your children to school until you are told not to. Do not try to go and live somewhere else. Do not use the roads for any unnecessary journey; they must be left free for troop movements even a long way from the district where actual fighting is taking place.

3. Will certain roads and railways be reserved for the use of the Military, even in areas far from the scene of action?

Yes, certain roads will have to be reserved for important troop movements; but such reservations should be only temporary. As far as possible, bus companies and railways will try to maintain essential public services, though it may be necessary to cut these down. Bicyclists and pedestrians may use the roads for journeys to work, unless instructed not to do so.

ADVICE AND ORDERS

4. Whom shall I ask for advice?

The police and A.R.P. wardens.

5. From whom shall I take orders?

In most cases from the police and A.R.P. wardens. But there may be times when you will have to take orders from the military and the Home Guard in uniform.

6. Is there any means by which I can tell that an order is a true order and not faked?

You will generally know your policeman and your A.R.P. wardens by sight, and can trust them. With a bit of common sense you can tell if a soldier is really British or only pretending to be so. If in doubt ask a policeman, or ask a soldier whom you know personally.

INSTRUCTIONS

7. What does it mean when the church bells are rung?

It is a warning to the local garrison that troops have been seen landing from the air in the neighbourhood of the church in question. Church bells will *not* be rung all over the country as a general warning that invasion has taken place. The ringing of church bells in one place will not be taken up in neighbouring churches.

8. Will instructions be given over the wireless?

Yes; so far as possible. But remember that the enemy can overhear any wireless message, so that the wireless cannot be used for instructions which might give him valuable information.

9. In what other ways will instructions be given?

Through the Press; by loudspeaker vans; and perhaps by leaflets and posters. But remember that genuine Government leaflets will be given to you only by the policeman, your A.R.P. warden or your postman; while genuine posters and instructions will be put up only on Ministry of Information notice boards and official sites, such as police stations, post offices, A.R.P. posts, town halls and schools.

FOOD

10. Should I try to lay in extra food?

No. If you have already laid in a stock of food, keep it for a real emergency; but do not add to it. The Government has made arrangements for food supplies.

NEWS

11. Will normal news services continue?

Yes. Careful plans have been made to enable newspapers and wireless broadcasts to carry on, and in case of need there are emergency measures which will bring you the news. But if there should be some temporary breakdown in news supply, it is very important that you should not listen to rumours nor pass them on, but should wait till real news comes through again. Do not use the telephones or send telegrams if you can possibly avoid it.

MOTOR-CARS

12. Should I put my car, lorry or motor-bicycle out of action?

Yes, when you are told to do so by the police, A.R.P. wardens or military; or when it is obvious that there is an immediate risk of its being seized by the enemy—then disable and hide your bicycle and destroy your maps.

13. How should it be put out of action?

Remove distributor head and leads and either empty the tank or remove the carburettor. If you don't know how to do this, find out now from your nearest garage. In the case of diesel engines remove the injection pump and connection. The parts removed must be hidden well away from the vehicle.

THE ENEMY

14. Should I defend myself against the enemy?

The enemy is not likely to turn aside to attack separate houses. If small parties are going about threatening persons and property in an area not under enemy control and come your way, you have the right of every man and woman to do what you can to protect yourself, your family and your home.

GIVE ALL THE HELP YOU CAN TO OUR TROOPS

Do not tell the enemy anything

Do not give him anything

Do not help him in any way

(55001) Wt. 46381/P1609 14,050,800 (2 kds.) 5/41 Hw. G.51

1940

CHAPTER I

A False Alarm

Plymouth

Sunday 8 September During the night – I do not know at what time, but it was still dark – I was woken up by a voice saying 'Members of the Home Guard – report for duty immediately.' It was a loudspeaker van going through the streets; I heard it getting alternately louder and softer as it went, until at last it passed out of hearing and I went to sleep again.

I was quite prepared to hear on the eight o'clock news that we had been invaded – though on thinking it over, I remembered that the church bells would have rung – but heard, instead, of a heavy all-night raid on London. A special bulletin at 10.15 a.m. stated that about 400 people were killed and 1,300 to 1,400 seriously injured. 88 German aircraft were shot down during the day. It has been quiet here for a few days, and it is hardly possible to realise that four hundred people were killed last night, only six hours' rail journey away.

Mrs. S. next door told us, laughing, that according to the newspaper man, 'They've landed everywhere but in this here road'. This was apparently what he had heard in the course of his round, and was absolute rubbish. When we[1] went out, however, we were somewhat perturbed to see a good many tin-hatted soldiers about, and barricades on the main roads – till we saw that the soldiers were pulling them down and not building them. It rained today for the first time in many weeks, so we picked two of our precious tomatoes to save them from getting battered. They are quite a good size. My lettuces seem to have survived the dry weather pretty well – probably due to their almost-daily drink of bath water. My peas are over now, but we have carrots, various cabbages, turnips and onions still coming along.

Monday 9 September This morning we read in the papers – which, although London had a 10-hour raid, were not more than about two

---

1. At this stage, 'we' means my parents and me.

hours late – that [church] bells were rung yesterday in various parts of the West Country and in Surrey. Somebody apparently went off the deep end and 'saw things'. However, I expect it was quite useful to have a practice.

We had intended to play tennis this morning, but it was so windy that we went into Plymouth instead. I bought a copy of *The Pilgrim's Progress* (4s.) – very extravagant! However, I compensated for it by buying some economy labels [for re-using envelopes]. I always seem to spend a lot of money if I get 'a drop of leaf', [the soldiers' and sailors' expression for leave] so it is just as well I don't get it so very often. It was quite pleasant to see people wearing the usual strange variety of clothes, after for so long seeing hardly anything but uniform. There is such a wonderful variation in face, as well as in dress, among civilians. I suppose it is because, being free to choose their own clothes, they accentuate their own peculiarities instead of more or less hiding them under uniform. To look at the shops, one could hardly tell there was a war, apart from notices about [air-raid] shelters and not using paper unless necessary. The grocers' shops are full and the windows of the drapers are equally full, with the colours and designs as bright as ever.

This afternoon I had another bath: it was cold at first but all right afterwards.

The casualties in the first mass attack on London have now been found to be fewer than it was thought – 306 and 1,300-odd [killed and injured]. I don't know that there is much point in giving the actual figures, so I don't think I will in future.

Tuesday 10 September Casualties in the second raid on London were nearly as heavy as in the first. No *Daily Telegraph* today and the *Daily Mail* arrived about two hours late. This morning I bicycled down to the War Aid Supply Depot with a bulging bundle of clothes for distribution. The weather was not good enough for tennis or swimming.

This afternoon we walked from Cornwood to Ivybridge across Hanger Down. There was a great deal of cloud over the moor and it drizzled once or twice, but not enough to spoil the walk. It was very enjoyable. Went without tea and had an omnibus meal when we got back.

Wednesday 11 September A fine day. I went to the Aquarium this morning. Two of the tanks were particularly interesting: one with mackerel, which swam all together to and fro very restlessly, and cuttle-fish, which are most repulsive. The next one had enormous lobsters, conger-eel, dog-fish and ballan wrasse. I had never realized before that there are amiable and unamiable fish. There was a big speckled wrasse, brilliantly spotted, who swam about very calmly and looked at me through the glass; but the other things were horrible. The conger – slow and deliberate in their movements, with cold flat eyes, and a dead sort of grey in colour, and the dogfish, which are so indecently sinuous! When one of the eels passed over the lobsters, they stuck out their antennae and passed them along its body. It withdrew backwards, swimming almost vertically up, its jaws opening and closing all the time. Then I thought I saw the gravel bottom move, but it was a turbot. And it really stretched and yawned. It hollowed its back stiffly, and opened its horny jaws so wide and so long that its head seemed almost to detach itself from its body. I should not like to be one of the little fish living in that tank. It was quite a relief to pass on to the next, where some silvery, benign-looking, cod were cruising rather aimlessly about, with a sapphirine gurnard, so called, I suppose, from its deep blue eyes – though there were some ugly-looking ray lying on the bottom. They don't seem to have the same breathing arrangements as other fish; instead of gills heaving, there were two little round holes on their backs opening and closing. Among the other specimens I liked the sleek grey mullet, various wrasse, starfish, and the irascible-looking three-bearded rockling, who scowled at me in a most ferocious way – considering he was not more than six inches long.

From the Hoe itself I watched a [Sunderland] flying-boat come in. I have seen them often before, but there is something fascinating about the way they glide down so slowly until at last they strike the water and send up a plume of white spray. I went on to the Barbican and back to the centre of the town by New Street [in fact one of the oldest in Plymouth, dating from the fifteenth century or earlier], where I encountered a smell I've never found anywhere except in HMS *Victory*, down near the keel. This was by Collier's wine-cellars. There is a place near here – or was up to a year or two ago – where they still make ships' biscuits by hand in a very old coal-fired oven. I once interviewed the baker and he gave me some of them. They were very hard, but quite good with cheese. [This was in my first job, where I was supposed to be learning the ropes as 'trainee' to a free-lance journalist]. I came home by tram, on the one remaining route (through Peverell), which makes a fair circuit of the town.

We have had a good many raids here – though I don't propose to mention them on the days when they occur, in case this might fall into the hands of a Fifth Columnist (why we don't call them by the good old name of traitor I can't imagine), but there was no sign of any damage on this long route.

I have made no mention of raids in London, but they have been going on all this week.

Terry[1] was to have arrived for seven days' leave at 1930: I went to the station to meet him at about 2000, having rung up to find out if the train was late. One came in at 2010, and another at 2030; but he wasn't in either, so I came home again. I have not heard anything dated later than Saturday.

Thursday 12 September A letter this morning from Terry, dated Sunday, saying that leave had been temporarily stopped and hoped it would be restored. I went to see his father and mother, who had heard nothing, but thought he had probably been delayed en route and did not seem worried. Other people are said to have taken twenty-four hours on the journey. Mrs. Deacon gave me some seed onions and leek plants, which were welcome, because onions were 8d a pound the other day.

No further news from Terry, so I conclude his leave has been definitely stopped. This afternoon Letitia[2] and I rather wasted in wandering round the shops – though we did buy some turnip and onion seed. It was chilly and unpleasant; and we had tea at Dingle's. There was a soldier with greasy black hair, a loose mouth and hard bold eyes, accompanied by a fat, fair, cow-like girl who appeared to be hanging on his words; the usual middle-aged shoppers; children, who looked (as usual) with interest at the inside of their cakes after the first bite; and one rather subdued-looking girl who for some reason caught my attention. Also a very attractive, large-eyed, dark-haired woman (who knew she was attractive, in a dainty and yet Slavonic way), with a vague fair woman, both of whom sat smoking cigarettes in long holders. Why that should seem an endeavour to attract attention I don't quite know, because they were quiet-mannered; but I had a distinct feeling that it was – and not on account of any inherent prejudice.

Mrs. Deacon rang up early this evening to know if we had any news, and is reported to be feeling anxious. Personally, I think (as I said before) that leave has been stopped – and I don't go beyond that. It is

1. Terry – not Terence – Deacon was a friend from childhood, and unofficial fiancé. His parents, George Harold and Elizabeth Ruth Deacon, who had a small shop, had reared a large family of clever children. Terry had been articled to a local solicitor, but this had been interrupted at the beginning of the War, when, as a member of the Territorial Army, he had been called up. Being a conscientious objector, he had joined the Royal Army Medical Corps – but his views changed later, as will appear. He continued his law studies with the help of a correspondence course, and passed his final in 1942.
2. Letitia – my mother. Years ago we had adopted the names of characters from L. du Garde Peach's *Toytown* stories, which used to be broadcast in the old Children's Hour. My father was the Mayor, my mother Letitia Lamb, Terry Ernest the Policeman, and I, for some odd reason, Captain 'Iggins the furniture remover. Another boy we knew, called Dennis, was obviously cast as Dennis the Dachshund.

disappointing, because I don't know when I shall get leave again, and it's very difficult to get our dates to fit, even approximately.

The trouble with keeping a diary is that I find myself deliberately collecting material for it, whereas I intended it merely to be an outlet for any stray ideas that occur to me. It seems a little ridiculous to find oneself looking on life as something to provide entries in a diary – especially at a time like this.

I should have mentioned that in his speech last night, Winston Churchill rather emphasized the possible imminence of invasion. It's a bit like the Fat Boy in Pickwick – 'I wants to make your flesh creep' – which I should say is by no means a bad thing in the circumstances. If a disaster is averted, or turns out to be not quite as bad as we expected, we seem to become unreasonably cheerful and perhaps complacent – so it's as well to keep us on the alert. (Somewhat obvious).

Friday 13 September A blustery day, which started in heavy rain and then cleared up.

This morning we went to Plymouth for week-end shopping.

A letter from Terry arrived this afternoon, dated Sunday, to say that his leave had been stopped – 'to give us ample warning'! So my explanation was correct.

I read a horrible thing in the paper the other day. A London woman said: 'They're making us suffer; I hope German women and children are being made to suffer too'. One feels sorry for her and can understand her saying it; but it is a dreadful thing, and I do not think the paper should have printed it. And there are letters saying we should 'wipe out' German towns. There are so many things wrong about it. It is merely revenge, which is barren of everything but hate – and there will be enough of that after the War without adding to it. Augustine of Hippo said, so many centuries ago, that the horror of war was not so much in the violent death of people, who must inevitably die in the course of nature, as in the release of hatred. It is terrible to think of so much force being spent in destruction – of life, buildings, ships, aeroplanes – and the waste of ingenuity, energy and material. If all this can be devoted to the present end, how much ought to be spent in preserving peace and improving things afterwards: as all this might have been, but for the War. It seems as if a kind of mass insanity has descended upon Europe, and perhaps the whole world.

To revert to the bombing of women and children. I think we lay too much stress on the mere sex. It is the bombing of civilians – especially children – that is the thing to be censured, surely. It is terrible to bomb anybody, even if he is armed from head to foot, but to attack the defenceless is cowardly. I shouldn't (I hope) ask for mercy on the sole ground of my sex (speaking as a class); I am to a certain extent responsible, having a vote, and serving in one capacity or another in the defences, even if it is only indirectly – and certainly wishing success to those defences – as much as any male civilian. If women are to have equal rights (which in fact they haven't, but are always asking for) they should, as far as possible, accept equal burdens. Can it be morally worse to kill a woman air-raid warden than a man? They are both doing the same job.

I suppose the 'women and children's' protagonists could get out of it by saying that as there are more women than men, the majority of civilians are women. But the fact remains that it is the bombing of civilians that they mean, or ought to mean. Children are on a different footing. It must leave a dreadful impression on a child's mind to see such things (apart from the ethical aspect) and to hear all round them nothing but war-talk – and to be brought up in an atmosphere of hate and alarm.

In the meantime let us keep our hands as clean as we can and do what we have to do rather to preserve our own people than to destroy those of Germany, which is a more effective as well as a more humane – or rather, less brutal – way of waging war, with as little hate as we may. It will be hard enough in any case for England and Germany to regard each other in a reasonably calm way after this is over.

I have been (and still am) re-reading *The Brothers Karamazov*. It seems quite a different book from what I thought when I first read it. It is a wonderful piece of work: the old man Fyodor is in my opinion the most extraordinary character, in terms of presentation, of any I've yet met. The thing that strikes me particularly is the detail, the variety, and 'depth' – in a plastic sense – of the portrait: it really is wonderful.

CHAPTER II

Engagement

Saturday 14 September I returned to duty this morning. [Weather permitting, this involved a bicycle ride to Mount Wise, some two miles away, where, in addition to the original offices of the Commander in Chief, part of one or two official residences had been taken over and an extension added in the form of wooden huts. Later the huts and at least part of the houses were burned down in air-raids.] My seven days seem to have passed very quickly, in spite of not very good weather and a general feeling of – not exactly unrest, but a kind of suppressed anxiety. The idea of imminent invasion is in the air, and the continual attacks on London are very dreadful. The famous buildings – St. Paul's and the various City churches that have been damaged, Buckingham Palace, Regent Street – seem to belong to everyone, not only to one city.

When there is an air raid at night, we go downstairs into a passage between the dining-room and the wall adjoining the next house. There was a door [leading to the garden] but we have had it walled in with concrete blocks, with a lighter section in the middle to let us get out if the other end were blocked. We keep a hammer and chisel ready. There are mattresses and cushions on the floor, and an extension light leads off from the hall. Each of us has a suitcase packed with a general selection of clothes, and we keep some more, that are not in constant use, hanging on the wall. I also make a point of bringing down the suit of uniform actually in use, with at least one shirt and a small bag with money and oddments. By day we cover the cases with rugs and cushions so that they can be used as seats; and at night we try to sleep. If the raid is a long one, we generally succeed and several times we have missed the all-clear siren. The steady blast is less penetrating than the 'warbling' note of the alarm, or 'alert' as they now call it; but we even managed to miss that once, when the wireless was making a lot of noise with atmospherics.

At first we used to expect to see the town very much knocked about after a raid, especially if we had actually heard any bombs; but after a time everyone has got used to it and now takes it with a calm which is almost horrible. The whole business is so cold: you hear a whistling and an explosion and anti-aircraft gunfire, and then you come out and go on where you left off. And somewhere you see a pile of rubbish where there was a house or a shop and you're told that people were killed there. And you hear, and carry on – deciding whether you will plant turnips or parsnips for next Spring, or something equally petty. I suppose it is a good thing: the nervous strain would be very great if it were not so, but it seems horrible that we can have settled down in this cold-blooded way to accepting raids and their consequences as part of ordinary life.

Before 18 June, when raids really began in earnest, I used to wake sometimes, hearing an aircraft, rather alarmed, and wonder if it was a German. And motor engines changing gear or going up hill used to sound like sirens, but now they don't; and having found that I'm not petrified with fright during a raid, I'm not so startled when the alarm does go. I'm not pretending to be heroic; in fact the only way I can be not frightened is not to think about it, except in a casual way; but at least I have learned not to think about it. At first it was the feeling that whatever you did – broadly speaking – nothing was going to save you from a direct hit, that got you down; but now one says, 'It's no good running away or getting excited', and that produces a kind of courage. Whatever you do you can't get out of it, so you might as well sit tight and look brave at least, even if you aren't really. I can't imagine ever getting worked up about missing a train or getting wet or any of those little things, after this.

Sunday 15 September I did not have to go on duty this morning, so I spent most of the time doing various things in the garden. We cut down and dug up an old genista which was more or less dead; it took about an hour and provided quite good exercise.

This afternoon Letitia and I, at my instigation, broke our custom of not going out on Sunday afternoon by setting out to walk from Colebrook to Roborough. We had walked nearly halfway when someone volunteered the information that people were being stopped by the soldiers further on, unless on business. We had to walk back, which was most annoying, though we did manage to vary the route by returning by another lane on to the road at some distance nearer Plymouth. It would have been a good walk, I think, if not interrupted.

According to the nine o'clock news, 165 German planes were brought down today (since increased to 185).

I have finished my sea-boot stockings, which I think I shall ask to have allocated to the Polish Navy. We have fighting with us now Poles and Czechs, both of whom are doing well in the air, French under General de

Gaulle[1], Belgians, Dutch and Norwegians. The Poles have, of course, been here longer than any – Naval units, that is.

Monday 16 September There have been some first-class rumours going about today, mostly on the theme of the invasion. A number of German soldiers, varying from 1,000 to 45,000 (!), is alleged to have been sunk on its way across; and 165 (very precise!) are said to have landed and been killed by the Home Guard. These were going round the town in various forms.

Mrs. Marks[2] rang up this evening because she had heard a bomb had been dropped near us (not true). Desmond has bicycled down from London and is going to stay here. Alfred has been given a clerical job because they found he wasn't up to manual labour . . .

This morning I had my first experience of telephoning in a gas mask, for practice. It sounded rather muffled, even to me, and was more than a little awkward, but seemed to work. I wish mine didn't make me feel as though I were being gently suffocated. It is not that I can't breathe, but that it is not pleasant to have one's face enclosed.

Wednesday 18 September I don't think anything worth recording happened yesterday. It was very windy and generally uncomfortable.

I acquired a tin hat today, so I am feeling very brave. It is rather heavy and seems to pull my hair – but I mustn't look a gift horse in the mouth – especially one of this nature. [At that time, when a warning was sounded, we used to go down to the cellar under the office and try to carry on with the work. The cellar was immaculately whitewashed, floored with thick linoleum, and was used as offices for the storage and amendment of confidential books, e.g. code and cypher tables.]

Three letters from Terry arrived this morning, dated Sunday, Monday and Tuesday of last week.

I am now knitting vests for 'bombees' – children. I think I shall give them to the local people, because London gets help from the Dominions and people everywhere – though the present need here is of course relatively small.

I do not seem to have much energy when I come home in the evenings nowadays. There are plenty of things I ought to do, but all that actually gets down is reading and a little knitting during news bulletins and air raids.

---

1. Charles de Gaulle (1890–1970): President of French Republic 1959–69.
2. This was a Liberal Jewish family whom we had first met on holiday in Cornwall some years before. Desmond was to have become a Rabbi, but was killed in the War.

Saturday 21 September I am afraid this doesn't get written up much now except at week-ends. There is not much time in the week: I don't get home till after 7, and by then I haven't a great deal of energy. [This was a period of great pressure, arising from the aftermath of the evacuation of the Low Countries and France.]

I had my first game of hockey this afternoon. It was very hot but very enjoyable. But for three Wrens (including myself), it was all men – a practice game. Afterwards we had tea in the pavilion, and I returned to duty, having been absent about twice as long as I had said I should be. However, it didn't seem to matter.

Sunday 22 September I had to go on duty this morning. It is a muggy, drizzly day, but not unpleasant.

Looking back over the past few months, it is quite interesting to see how my outlook has changed. At the capitulation of France I felt most depressed and was principally concerned with the various forms of violent death I might meet. My main idea was that I did not want to be bombed or machine-gunned – I had a particular aversion for the latter; and that life, thought not exactly joyous, was extremely desirable. From that I slowly advanced to the idea that life would not be so desirable if we should happen not to win, and that in that event it wouldn't much matter whether I was alive or not, though I wanted to be there if we did win. Now, however, I feel (or at least I hope I do, in my stronger moments) that my personal fate matters precisely nothing, so long as we defeat Germany. That is logically obvious; but it's a bit hard to make up one's mind to it, though I realize that if we went under, it would be the end of European civilization as we have known it, and many years – even centuries – would have to pass before its rebirth. Just lately I have realized it more vividly, and that has made me have rather less regard for my unimportant self.

The particular point about death by bombing that is so dreadful is its futility. If one could feel that by risking one's life one could save someone or something of importance, it would not be quite so bad: it would be an active sacrifice, not a merely passive wiping-out process; but it is difficult to feel that one is achieving any great good by being blown to bits in a cellar. In the aggregate, of course, it is important that we should be able to face the prospect – but it does not offer any satisfaction to one's personal vanity.

Tuesday 24 September A telegram arrived this evening saying that Terry was coming home on leave on Thursday. Perhaps he'll get here this time!

The papers, just now, especially the *Daily Mail*, are printing numerous letters demanding the bombardment of non-military objectives in Germany. This is absurd. It is only a blind wish for revenge and in my opinion is not based on any rational idea. The only thing that will stop the Germans from bombing non-military objectives will be the lack of power to do so: and the way to deprive them of it is not to bomb haphazardly and goad them to possibly worse things, but to attack their military strength.

Thursday 26 September Terry was to have arrived at 1930; but when I rang up the railway (twice) earlier in the evening they couldn't tell me when [the train] would be in. So I gave up the idea of meeting him and went straight to his house. Shirley [his youngest sister] rang up again and was told that it should arrive about 2030. Berenice [an older sister] very kindly ran me down in the car – in spite of the fact that the petrol tank registered empty: the end of the month is usually a bit like that! [On account of petrol rationing]. We got there about 2020. There were a lot of soldiers about and the blue light wasn't very clear, so we found ourselves gazing earnestly into the faces of complete strangers. [Lights had to be dimmed by blue paint as part of air raid precautions.] Then the searchlights started – we could hear a plane – and practically all the station lights were turned out. We both had tin hats, but we were hoping there wouldn't be a warning, because if we had taken shelter in the station dug-out, we might have missed the train. However, it blew over.

Berenice takes the precaution of tying a label on the steering wheel saying that the car is immobilized – having once had part of her engine removed by an enthusiastic constable. [Parked cars had to be immobilized, so as not to be available to unsuitable people, such as invading parachutists.]

According to a chalked-up notice, the train was 70 minutes late, but it didn't arrive until 2100. Terry had his usual vast load of equipment, and had to crawl into the car on hands and knees. [Oddly, this seemed easier than removing the pack] He had been travelling since about 0700.

Friday 27 September This morning I had an anti-typhoid inoculation consisting of what looked like dirty, or rather, cloudy, water. [This was a routine precaution for all Service personnel, against the risk that water supplies might be polluted as a result of bombing.] It was all right at the time but after bicycling home to lunch I began to feel rather conscious of my arm. By evening I was feeling hot and uncomfortable, and was very glad to go home early. Terry suggested that we might be engaged this evening. He had mentioned it to me yesterday, but this was *coram publico*.

Saturday 28 September I did not feel up to going on duty this morning; in fact I stayed in bed till about 1330. Terry and I then went to Plymouth to get the ring, which was very nice. I still felt rather ache-y, but not too bad. [The effect of the inoculation – plus some inexplicable embarrassment – must be the reason for this very lack-lustre account of the engagement. And of course for Terry and me it was only the announcement of something we had regarded as settled while we were still at school.]

Sunday 29 September I did not have to go on duty this morning, so Terry and I went to his house to show the ring. We spent some time there watching [his sister] Edna's guinea-pigs and mice [kept as models for painting] and talking to the family.

This evening Letitia rang up Terry's mother and persuaded her and Mr. Deacon to come here – I don't quite know why – but they came and everybody talked about odd things. They all seem very pleased about the engagement.

Monday 30 September Terry is coming to tea each day, but as I don't usually get home till about 7, the evenings seem very short. It was a pity his earlier leave was cancelled.

CHAPTER III

Selection Board

Tuesday 1 October I was informed today that I have to go to London for an Officers' [Selection] Board on Friday. It would have been much nicer if it could have been Thursday, so that I could have travelled with Terry. However, it can't be helped. I hope to go and return the same day, if the trains permit. A Wren is being lent to take my place while I am away; but I do not know if she will be the permanent relief.

Wednesday 2 October I had quite a strenuous day telling [Wren] Chapman what to do; it's much more tiring explaining things to other people than doing them oneself.

The end of Terry's leave seems to have come very quickly.

Thursday 3 October Terry came to breakfast this morning; he caught the 1230 train, so he was able to walk down to Mount Wise with me. His mother rang later with a message to say how sorry he was to go.

I was given this afternoon off, which was very welcome; I have a good many things to do. This morning I acquired a uniform hat, which is not exactly chic. [This was the original blue drill pull-on affair, which was only then beginning to be available: later, Wrens wore round caps, like the sailors' but soft. Officers wore tricornes.] There are a few other Wrens going up to-morrow: it will be better than travelling completely solo.

Friday 4 October I left North Road Station at 0830, with three other Wrens (Dane, Coates and Dean.)[1] We split up into two parties, Dean and I travelling together. We had the compartment to ourselves until Taunton. From there on there were a Cockney sailor and his rather frightened-looking young wife, a very tough and weather-beaten airman, a Regular Army staff-sergeant, a civilian with an ARP [Air Raid Precaution] badge and an elaborately-dressed middle-aged woman who provided a good deal of entertainment. She made conversation in a mildly flirtatious way with the sailor and soldier, the latter of whom talked very good sense

---

1. Later Third Officer P.D. Dane, Second Officer E.D. Coates and Second Officer R.M. (or A) Dean (identification uncertain).

about the War – in contrast to her somewhat second-hand and very easily shaken opinions. She got out at Westbury, and it seemed quite quiet without her.

We had hoped to get lunch, but omitted to get tickets for it, and when we reached the dining car, after a good deal of climbing over soldiers in the corridor, it was full. To make sure of having something, Dean got out at Reading and bought some rolls with slices of sausage inside. We had two each, and they were very welcome; it was then 1300, and we had had breakfast about 0730.

As the train was running into London, the guard came along to warn us that there was an air-raid in progress. We could hear gunfire, but not very near, as far as we could tell. At Paddington we hoped to be able to wash and change our collars, but they wouldn't let us on account of the raid. It seemed rather silly, especially as the wash-place was underground; and we were not too pleased, because by that time we were feeling pretty hot and tired, and more than a little grubby. The Tube, apparently, was not running for some reason or other (I don't think it had been damaged), so we had to take a taxi. It was about 1430; the train was half an hour late, and we were due at WRNS Office at 1500.

We managed to get a taxi on the station and I was glad we hadn't been able to go by tube. [This was my first visit to London since the age of three.] It was a wonderful drive, across Hyde Park, past Buckingham Palace and the Mall, to Admiralty Arch, at the corner of Trafalgar Square. The guns were going intermittently all this time. When we reached Charing Cross, the door was shut – apparently everyone had gone to ground; but fortunately there was a Wren there who belonged to the Office. She took us over to the Admiralty shelter, where there were a number of Wrens, including one or two officers. They rang up to say we had arrived and after a little while someone came over to fetch us. The WRNS office were very kind, and let us wash and change our collars, which was a great relief. They also gave us cups of tea. Everyone seemed to look on us as the heroines of the occasion, having come so far.

The Board consisted of four – the Director[1], Deputy Director[2], and two other officers[3] – sitting in a small room, so that the atmosphere was quite friendly. The Director did most of the questioning – perfectly straightforward questions about my work, and what I did before joining the WRNS, and put so quickly that one forgot to be self-conscious.

---

1. Dame Vera Laughton Mathews DBE.
2. Miss E.M. Goodenough CBE.
3. One was the Staff Officer, Lady Cholmondeley: the Dowager Marchioness of Cholmondeley CBE.

We hoped to be able to see Miss Woollcombe[1], who used to be Chief Officer at Plymouth, but unfortunately she was busy; so we went out to have a look at London. I could have been quite happy to stand in Trafalgar Square and stare, or even more to go back the way we had come. I saw, or thought I saw, a glimpse of the Houses of Parliament. But Dean wanted to see the shops, so we wandered up the Strand. We found a Lyons' cafe, and went in to have tea. The waiter was just able to serve us when they announced that the raid was overhead and stopped the service. The band went on playing, however, and nobody seemed to take much notice. The waiter treated us to a brief lecture on the folly of not going to bed, or at least to sleep, when there were night air-raids. After a little while we went out. The streets were quite full; apparently it was more or less a rush-hour. It was raining quite hard now.

We got to one big building that looked rather interesting, so Dean asked a newspaper man what it was. 'I don't know,' he said. She laughed and asked if he thought she was a Fifth Columnist. A policeman on the gate was a little less cautious. He said 'Well, Miss, have you ever heard of Somerset House? This is where you come when you're born and when you die,' and so on. There was one large hole in the road further on, presumably the work of the Luftwaffe. Soon afterwards we took a taxi back to Paddington, and while we were on the way, the 'alert' went again – about half an hour after the all-clear. The driver was disgusted and mimicked it, saying, 'There it goes again'. He also told us not to be frightened if we heard gunfire! On the way back we drove through Regent Street, where some of the shops were rather knocked about, but it remains an impressive street.

We decided to pay the excess fare and travel first-class, in the hope of getting some sleep, or at least of being comfortable. Just as the train was leaving the station (at 1830), an attendant said the first dinner was ready. We got up very quickly and made a straight line for the dining-car, feeling extremely hungry after our scanty lunch and tea. It was a very good dinner, or at least seemed so to us. At our table there was a Mercantile Marine [then so named] officer whose ship had been sunk by a bomb. He was on his way to Bristol for the week-end, hoping to see for the first time his second daughter, aged two months. The meal lasted an hour and made a pleasant break. Just before we reached Bristol, the Mercantile Marine officer looked into our compartment for a farewell chat; and then we heard the sirens go. The lights were turned off, and for some reason the train stopped.

---

1. Later a Director WRNS; Dame Jocelyn Woollcombe DBE.

We stood in the corridor to look out but couldn't see anything. When we finally stopped at Bristol Station, we had to get out and go up to the front of the train, and got into a compartment where there was a post-captain, an RAF officer and a civilian. The captain, whose name was Foster[1], said he had spoken to Captain Lush[2] recently on the telephone.

The RAF man was a Spitfire pilot, and had been wounded in the leg when his machine was shot down. His foot was in plaster, on which some of his friends had signed their names during a party in the hospital. He had just swapped one of his buttons for a Polish one – which is apparently a custom: he said one officer had one button each of Polish, Belgian, Czech, French and British.

Everyone took a great interest in us and wished us retrospective good luck. They let us read their papers, so we handed round chocolate and fudge.

After what seemed like hours in the darkness, the train stopped. I said 'This must be Taunton'; actually it was Weston-super-Mare. We began to feel a bit bored after that. F/O Marples kept saying he would like some bacon and eggs; but I think I should have preferred some sleep. From Newton Abbot we had the compartment to ourselves and lay down on the seats (there aren't any sleeping coaches now), but couldn't sleep. We arrived at North Road Station at 0415 – three-and-a-quarter hours late. There was only one taxi to be had, so we all four got into it – having picked up the others again – and went round dropping people at their houses. I finally got to bed at 5, and didn't wake, except for an interruption, till 1230, when I felt very ready for my lunch, not having had breakfast. I seemed to have been fussing about food ever since about 1200 on the previous day. I got up about 1330 and went out, though feeling somewhat lazy. At teatime Captain Lush, or rather [Wren], Chapman, rang up to say I needn't go in till Monday – of which I was very glad.

Sunday 6 October Wet, windy and quite restful. I think I'm now clean, after two baths and washing my hair. I was quite filthy after the double journey. [The reason was smuts from the steam locomotive.]

Monday 7 October This morning I had my second instalment of anti-typhoid. My arm had swollen considerably by bed-time, and I seemed to have most impressive biceps. Very stiff, but apparently no general effects. I had a letter from Terry saying he's arrived back safely.

1. Perhaps Captain F.A.P. Foster.
2. Captain E.C. Lush CB, whose writer (secretary) I was.

Tuesday 8 October I didn't sleep very well; but apart from a stiff arm and a certain lack of interest in life, I feel normal and put in an ordinary day's work. People keep asking me when I shall be leaving. . .

Friday 11 October It was announced today that St. Paul's Cathedral had been hit by a bomb, which wrecked the high altar and made a hole in the roof, but fortunately did not damage the dome or the main structure. It is a great pity. The papers had photographs – and very striking they were. The light from the hole in the roof showed up the carving and mural paintings very clearly, shining down on the heap of rubble where the altar had been.

Saturday 12 October . . . I have been accepted [as an officer cadet] and am to start cypher training as soon as a relief can be found. Chapman is apparently not coming, which means I shall have to train someone all over again – and this time right from the beginning, as the girl who is to be sent 'on approval' is new to the Service.

This afternoon I had a pleasant game of hockey at Royal Naval Barracks (Mount Wise against RNB Wrens). We won 11–1, playing ten-a-side, which was comparatively restful after our scratch games of about seven-a-side.

Tuesday 15 October It was announced in the 9 o'clock news today that HMS *Ajax* has sunk three Italian destroyers in two engagements . . . She was already famous for her share in the Battle of the River Plate, with *Exeter* and *Achilles*, in December 1939. *Ajax* and *Exeter* came into Plymouth on their return from the American Station [in January and February 1940] and on both occasions we were allowed to go on to the Admiral's lawn and watch. Winston Churchill, Sir John Simon[1], and various local celebrities came down to welcome *Exeter*.

At the suggestion of Captain Lush, I am to take a day off to-morrow, so that he can see how my relief (name of Harding) is progressing.

We had a game of mixed hockey at 1730. Very good exercise.

Friday 18 October A quaint little man came into the office today who had written a song called 'For Liberty' or something like that, and recited it. He said he'd written it under his stairs in an air raid, saying to his daughter, 'Give me a pencil and paper – I've got words coming'. I must say it sounded like it, being of a genuine ballyhoo make.

---

1. Sir John Simon (1873–1954), Chancellor of the Exchequer: later Viscount Simon.

I am to start cypher training on Monday. [Members of the WRNS undertook a great variety of shore-based jobs. In addition to the obvious categories, like writers i.e. stenographers and clerks, cooks and stewards and so on, there were drivers, at first limited to cars, but later taking on larger vehicles, including three-ton lorries. A tremendous number were employed in communications – ratings as coders (handling 'confidential' signals) and officers as cypherers (handling 'secret' and 'top secret' signals), helping with the whole complicated process of transmitting and receiving orders and information to and from ships at sea and overseas bases. As time went on, more and more work was taken over by the WRNS – as despatch riders, boats' crews, wireless telegraphists, aircraft mechanics, catering officers and even a few 'Flag Lieutenants', re-named Personal Assistants, to Commanders in Chief at major bases. By the end of the War the list included radar detection finders, cinema operators, meteorological officers, recruiters, submarine attack teacher operators, bomb range markers, vision testers, ciné gun assessors, anti-aircraft target operators, tailoresses, routing officers, and orthoptists[1]. Many served abroad, and some were lost at sea on the outward voyage. A few cypher officers served on board the 'Monsters' – liners like the *Queen Mary* and *Queen Elizabeth*, which were being used as troop transports.]

---

1. Stuart Mason.

CHAPTER IV

Officer Cadet

Saturday 19 October I said good-bye to Captain Lush today. He thanked me (!) and was very nice about it. I am very sorry to leave: I have liked the job so well, and I'm sure I shall miss the 'social life' attached to it.

[During the summer, after the fall of France, we had had a great deal to do with Allied naval people and others who had escaped in one way or another. There were the three Polish destroyers – *Burza*, *Grom* and *Blyskawica* – which had escaped from Gdynia when Poland was overrun in 1939 and made their way to France and then to England in 1940. Their officers learned to speak fluent English in about two weeks and were splendid people. They had the charming custom of greeting a woman (if married) by kissing her hand. The Poles were greatly admired for their courage and determination; later, when more had arrived, they were provided with British ships, which they manned and which, with their own destroyers, joined British operational units, ultimately with a Pole as Senior Officer. They had had extraordinary experiences: one officer from the south of Poland had served in the Austrian Fleet Air Arm, or equivalent, in the First World War, and bombed the French battleship *Paris*, which was now lying in Devonport Dockyard as an Allied vessel. The merchant ship *Gdynia* served as their depot ship for a time; later the former United Services Orphanage building in Devonport became the Polish Naval Barracks.

There was a Dutch merchant from Amsterdam, who had been rescued by the Royal Navy and insisted on showing his gratitude by writing a cheque, improvised on a sheet of plain paper, for a substantial sum to go to welfare funds. There were Free French, Belgians (who surprisingly found it easier to speak English than French), and of course many British people. Plymouth Sound was filled with ships and small craft of every description, probably something like two hundred at the peak. One day a hot meal from the naval kitchens at Devonport was served to everyone in every vessel: probably the first proper food that many of them had had for more than a week – and a major feat of organization.

Nearly every morning there would be a group of 'gallant Allies' of one or more nationalities on the doorstep waiting for the office to open – wanting help, information or an ear into which to pour a complaint. One event which caused a good deal of indignation was the removal, under Naval escort and without warning to their (mostly civilian) commanders, of a number of assorted Belgian small craft from Plymouth Sound to Brixham.

Apparently the first the Belgians knew of this was next morning, when they saw their boats were no longer in the Sound. Feelings ran high, and fairly pointed observations were made, to the effect that the Navy had been indulging in piracy and that financial compensation would be required. However, it was explained by various senior officers that there was a good reason for the sudden action, and that the boats would be restored to their rightful owners – and gradually the temperature returned to normal. [Years later, Captain Lush wrote: 'When I think of the huge staffs which subsequently developed, it gives me some satisfaction to reflect that the two of us in that ground floor office at Mount Wise House – always with the advice and assistance of Captain Ayre[1] – laid a good foundation for all that was to follow.']

Sunday 20 October [My twenty-third birthday] Terry sent me a lovely Swedish glass vase. I was also given André Maurois' *The Battle of France.* It is strange to read of the state of things in France at this time last year: and to look back at our attitudes of mind. Last Christmas Day we heard British soldiers broadcasting from the Maginot Line [the French system of fortifications along the German frontier], and French too. So much has happened since then that we could not have thought possible if anyone had foretold it: Norway, Denmark, Holland, Belgium and France. Poland had already been overrun. A Pole on the wireless the other day talked about the siege of Warsaw. There were no anti-aircraft defences and the ammunition ran out, while the city was bombarded from the ground as well as the air. It was terrible. Looking back it seems almost worse than at the time, though even then it seemed heart-rending. There have been such things in this War that I think we have lost the power to feel surprise, and we shall never again be able to fuss about minor annoyances. . .

I can hear a choir on somebody's wireless singing 'The King of Love' to the nice tune, soft and pleasing.

Miss Bessie[2] came to tea this afternoon, looking just the same as ever, and with her usual fund of news. This evening *The Barretts of Wimpole Street* was broadcast; quite well done, but it is not what I should call a great play.

---

1. Paymaster Captain L.C.E. Ayre OBE (later CBE), then Port Accountant Officer.
2. Miss B. Basden-Smith, my former headmistress: for some reason she was always known as Miss Bessie.

Monday 21 October I had to go and see the Secretary[1] this morning before starting my training, but didn't actually begin work till 1600, leaving at 2300. The work doesn't seem very abstruse.

[The cypher office and other operational sections were at that time housed in Egg Buckland Keep, one of the 'Palmerston' forts built round south-coast ports about 1860, when invasion by the French was feared. Semi-underground, it had numerous drawbacks, one of the most obvious being the absence of sanitation. This meant that if need arose, one had to go out across the drawbridge like a surface air-raid shelter; not difficult by day, but not so simple at night, since there was no lighting, as required by air-raid precautions. However, the Royal Marine sentry was always most helpful, politely shining his torch on the ground and leading one to the entrance.

The cypher office was immediately over the boiler, which produced strong, but presumably not noxious, fumes, since no-one seemed any the worse. Later the Area Combined Headquarters were transferred back to Mount Wise, in purpose-built accommodation more or less underground, known as the Moat.]

At least one of the Wrens who went to London with me was turned down; another is still in her old job; and one apparently has not yet heard. One of the Wrens on duty with me was at WRNS Headquarters for the same selection board as I, and has been transferred here since. There is a girl called Phillida Coode, who I believe was at Holt Corner [School, later re-named The Holt, at Alverstoke, Hampshire] with me, but I'm not sure.

Friday 25 October Mrs. Dent[2] told me today I am to be in her watch, starting about November 6. It is the most pleasant one, I think. Till then I carry on working 1100–2300 each day.

I asked Coode today about Holt Corner, and found that she was there – rather a curious coincidence.

Saturday 26 October We have had a fair number of raids this week, but not serious. We don't take so much notice of them now: the warning is to be regarded as an 'alert', and one carries on until the 'take cover' warning or until there is some noise. It is a much better scheme.

I had a pleasant walk this morning across the fields to Woodland Fort, Whitleigh and Higher St. Budeaux [on the outskirts of Plymouth].

---

1. Paymaster Captain J. Dent, Secretary to the Commander in Chief. As chief administrative officer he was responsible for appointments and for giving the mandatory warning about the Official Secrets Act.
2. Second Officer Mrs. Betty Dent, wife of Captain Dent.

Monday 28 October This morning (0300) Italy presented an ultimatum to Greece.

Sunday 3 November British naval forces have now landed in Greece [actually Crete] and . . . it seems that the Greeks are resisting with determination, and have even advanced a few miles into Albania.

I started work with Mrs. Dent's watch from today, and go on duty at 2300 till 0800. It is quite a relief to get settled: constantly changing [through working the same hours each day, while the normal watches rotated] was rather tiresome, because each watch has slightly different ways. Also I may be able to get some hockey now.

I went to see Captain Lush yesterday afternoon. He was as nice as ever.

My bundle of knitting for bombed babies is finished; but I am holding on to it until Letitia has completed the job of cutting down some old underclothes for the same purposes. I am glad I started when I did; a good many welfare organizations are appealing for clothes now, principally in London, of course.

Tuesday 5 November After a day at home (half of it in bed) – I went on duty 0800–1600 today. Milehouse [a neighbouring road junction] at 0730 was busier than I have seen it in daylight for a very long time. I had not realized there were so many people about at that hour.

In spite of the fact that bonfires and fireworks are not allowed, children have been going round the streets demanding 'Penny for the guy'. I can't imagine what they're going to do with them. It seems so frivolous to be begging in that way in these days of strenuous saving and 'Spitfire funds' and things of that sort.

Sunday 10 November Neville Chamberlain[1] has died. It seems a long time ago (1938) that he went to Godesberg and Munich to see Hitler about Czechoslovakia and came back with 'Peace in our time'.

Wednesday 13 November . . .The mornings are getting very dark and cold now; it was decided not to change over from 'Summer Time, but to leave the clocks advanced one hour, presumably for the duration.

Terry has now been sent to Yorkshire.

---

1. Arthur Neville Chamberlain (1869–1940), Prime Minister 1937 to May 1940, when he was succeeded by Winston Churchill.

Friday 15 November . . .Coventry was heavily bombed last night. It is estimated that the casualties may be something like 1,000; and the cathedral (14th century) was destroyed.

Tuesday 19 November . . .During the past few days Hitler has had interviews with Molotov[1], Ciano[2], and King Boris of Bulgaria. Incidentally he and Molotov are the only ministers of those concerned to whom the BBC gives a handle to their names. They got very tough on the day War was declared, and started saying Hitler, Ribbentrop etc. – very rude!

---

1. Vyacheslav Mikhailovitch Molotov (1890–1986) Foreign Commissar; later Deputy Premier of USSR.
2. Galeazzo Ciano (1903–44), Foreign Minister of Italy 1936–43. Found guilty of treason by the Fascists and shot 1944.

CHAPTER V

Officers' Training Course, R.N. College, Greenwich

25 November to 7 December I was told on Wednesday (20th) that I was to go to Greenwich for a course, and felt rather annoyed at first, but became reconciled to the idea later, especially as people who had been told me it was quite pleasant. It was quite a flap getting ready – I don't know why. I left North Road Station at 0830 on Monday 25th and reached London about 1430 – only half an hour late. From Paddington we took a taxi to Greenwich, as we had missed the connection we were told to catch. There were five of us from Plymouth – McKinlay, Rafarel, Rigg, Tuke and myself ... [A photograph of this (21st) course, in the archives of the National Maritime Museum, lists only the surnames; the full particulars cannot now be traced. Some records were probably lost when part of the R.N. College was bombed.

The list, supplemented by details from Navy Lists for subsequent years, is as follows:-

L.M.B. Acfield (Third Officer)
E.D. Cameron
Mrs. J.B. Crockart
K.R. Elliston (Third Officer)
B.J. Faber
D. Gascoigne
A.D. Hawkins (the present writer)
E.M. Ives
M.S. Johnstone
B.M. Kent
*Mrs. D.L.S. King (Third Officer)
M.B.T. Lawman
D. Lisle
A.E. McCallum

M.N. McKinlay
*M.M. Oldham (Third Officer)
*D.E. Pascoe
K.M.F. Piddocke
M.P. Pilley
R.G.M. Pope
Mrs. F.M. Rafarel
*M.E. Rigg
*A.M. Ritchie (Third Officer)
– Totton (not traced: Third Officer)
*Mrs. W.M.J. Tuke (Third Officer)
E.F. Walker

*Identification uncertain

We lived in Queen Anne Block, which is shared between the OTC and the WRNS Training Depot; and had our meals in the Painted Hall, which,

The Painted Hall, Greenwich.
By courtesy of The Greenwich Foundation for the Royal Naval College.

since 1939, has been used as the officers' mess. The Superintendent OTC was Miss French[1], who was very charming. After supper (dinner was off during the Blitzkrieg) we had to change into trousers (or other ARP clothes) in readiness for going to earth if necessary, even though the sirens had not always sounded. In fact there was no warning during Monday and Monday night; but all the same we slept in the cellar on mattresses, with the bedding from our cabins.

In the morning we usually had two lectures, either by WRNS or Naval officers, and occasionally by people from the Ministry of Information. Some of these were very interesting – particularly on Economic Warfare – and several from Naval Affairs. Normally we had three-quarters of an hour squad drill after lunch, under two Sergeants of Royal Marines, one of whom (Mann, who drilled the squad I was in) was quite a comic character – but on [the first] Tuesday afternoon they took us round the College, which is a lovely place. Our rooms in Queen Anne Block overlooked the river, where there were all kinds of ships passing. I particularly liked the sailing barges: I had not realized there were still so many of them in use. There were a good number of cargo ships and tugs, and occasionally naval patrol boats. The air was full of noise – throbbing propellers and riveting in a yard near at hand, and a good many unidentifiable sounds. We had quite a good view of the industrial part of the river; and there seemed to be a good many factories on the other side.

The Director came down for tea and ping-pong – at which she is pretty good – on the first Friday and again a week later, with Lady Cholmondeley and Mrs. Laybourne[2], for the passing-out board. Everyone did pass out all right, except a Petty Officer coder from Greenock who fainted [one evening during the course] when a big gun near at hand went off. [Everyone was sorry about that, because it was clear to us that she was tired and run down through overwork, and we hoped she would be given another chance.] Cecil Beaton came down one day and photographed some of the people he considered 'photogenic'. I was not among them – luckily.

There was a pea-soup fog on the Saturday, and I went for a walk by myself down the Woolwich Road. Greenwich struck me as being very old-fashioned – many of the shops had only gaslight – and most of the people seemed to be old. There was rather a scrooge-y atmosphere throughout, I thought. One day Rafarel and I went into a small stationer's shop for some postcards. It was very dark inside, with no

1. Miss E.N. French OBE.
2. First Officer Mrs. H.D. Laybourne.

artificial light. A queer little old woman, rather like a mole, came out and began to grope about on the shelves. She was apparently blind. It was almost eerie. I saw a thing I'd never seen before – a cats' meat stall, labelled 'Pussy's Butcher'. It also sold embrocation – rather a good combination, I should think.

Most of the houses are very small, built of yellowish brick turned black by time, and a good many of them had been damaged, to varying extents, by bombs. They had been pitted by flying bits, but were patched up, and a good proportion were apparently still in use. It was rather pathetic – they were so tiny and dismal, and so stuffily furnished in an old-fashioned way, I find it hard to describe. But I associate it with stuffed birds under glass, black sideboard-whatnots, and tea-caddies painted with close black and orange patterns. People, however, were busy shopping, and the little sweet-shops had their windows full of shiny Christmas 'novelties'. People like this are so phlegmatic; probably from the time they begin to think to when they die they have never had a thought above the routine of everyday life – and it is just that lack of imagination and susceptibility that enables them to put up with the things they now have to bear.

My walk was, in a way, depressing, but I enjoyed it. That sounds morbid – but it was interesting to me because it was so different from anything I had seen before – and not as a mere impartial observer.

On Sunday we went to Mattins in the College chapel. It was the shortest service I have ever been to – no psalms, and only bits of the canticles and hymns; rather as if everyone was in a hurry to go. Afterwards I went for a walk in Greenwich Park. The fog persisted, though not so thick, and there was a heavy white frost. The little toy-yacht pond was frozen over. It was rather lovely, with the grass completely white, and the old trees black against it in the fog. One couldn't see more than about thirty to fifty yards ahead, but the murmur of traffic and the usual noises went on. The Enclosure was the best part, and I saw some of the deer, and the ducks diving in the ornamental lake. I had previously been to the Observatory (outside only), from which one had the best view of the College and the Queen's House.

On the last day (Friday) we had to perform some squad drill before the Director in a bitter cold wind. She called out a few people in turn to take charge, but not me. The Board took up the rest of the day till tea-time, when we visited the Depot. WRNS ratings are trained there as wireless operators, stewards, cooks, and various other rates. It is a big place, and part of the old Palace of Placentia is still to be seen in the cellars.

A thing I forgot to mention was that every night after we had gone to bed underground [lying in rows on our mattresses], the Commander of the College (D'oyley[1] by name), attended by the two sergeants, came round to say goodnight. The real reason was presumably to see that everyone was in the right place, but it seemed to be rather a joke.

There was one lecture on Saturday before we left. Rafarel and I left Paddington at 1330 and reached Plymouth within about half an hour of the expected time – without incident. Two things make Plymouth seem particularly attractive: the clean air and the soft water. At Greenwich, though we could get daily baths, I never felt clean. The water was so hard, it was difficult to get really well soaped.

During the time I was away, there were heavy raids on Southampton (twice) and one rather bad one at Plymouth; but we had it reasonably quiet in London.

Monday 9 December This morning I reported to WRNS Office, where I was able to see Mrs. Welby[2]. The Director had told me she could not give me approval to get my uniform until she received my cyphering certificate, which she told me to hasten. This I endeavoured to do. 'A' watch was on from 2300 to 0800, but I did not have to go on duty till a.m. Wednesday. I put in a couple of hours' practice on a teleprinter on Tuesday, however.

I ordered my uniform from Gieves later on Monday, thinking it safe.

Monday 16 December This morning I had the first fitting of my uniform, which I think will be good when it is finished.

We are being asked to post all Christmas parcels and letters by Wednesday. For the first time (I suppose) the GPO are employing women as temporary deliverers, and soldiers are helping in the Post Office itself. Letters are rather slow, especially Terry's from Barnsley.

Tuesday 17 December Tonight I should have been on duty, but there was a spare night-off, which fell to me by chance (out of a hat in fact). I shall also get time off from Thursday 1630 to Monday 1800 – not leave, but a wangle which is going to be worked for everyone near Christmas.

We had a letter from Dennis[3], who is now at Portsmouth doing his courses as a Sub-lieutenant, after having been in the Mediterranean and at

1. Commander J.R. D'oyley.
2. Mrs. E.V. Welby CBE, Superintendent WRNS, Plymouth.
3. Later Dr. D.J.R.F. Nash, MRCS, LRCP.

the evacuation of Somaliland. He expects to go back to sea about February.

Tuesday 24 December The Minister of Food announced a little while ago that he would import no more fruit of any sort except a limited quantity of oranges, and no more canned fruit. It is, however, still possible to buy the latter, though naturally most shops will not sell more than one can of each kind to any one person. During the past few days we have not been able to get oranges, though this morning we missed some by only about one place in the [queue]. This afternoon we were able to get a dozen from a little shop nearby.

It may be of some interest to give some idea of the food we had for Christmas, in view of the shortage that Hitler declares we are suffering. The Market was full of poultry and vegetables, with more apples than I have ever seen in December, and grapefruit and lemons and nuts – but not oranges. We had a huge turkey (for us) – 12 pounds, costing about 30 shillings – and a small piece of bacon, with sprouts and celery and potatoes. This year we did not make pukka Christmas puddings, but had a very good substitute in the form of a boiled pudding containing eggs, raisins and spice. We bought a box of a pound of Australian muscatels for 1/10d, which wasn't really dear, considering the circumstances, and a few days ago we were able to get some onions – the first for a good many weeks. Lemons are plentiful now, after having been unobtainable.

A large parcel arrived this morning for me from Terry. Inside its many wrappings was a glass dish with a chromium-plated stand, which had travelled quite well, but for one tiny chip. It had taken four days to come from Barnsley. [This was an extraordinary object and I never discovered what it was meant for.] I went to see Terry's mother in the morning; being on duty from 1600 to 2300 prevented me from going in the evening as I had done before. She gave me two linen trolley-cloths – so I am collecting quite a bottom drawer!

Wednesday 25 December The King broadcast this afternoon, as he did last year on Christmas Day – though before the War he had said that he did not intend to do so because it was so closely associated with George V.

There were no air-raids on either England or Germany last night. As usual there was one postal delivery, but nothing came except a week-old letter from Terry.

Up to now we had had only electric heating, but today it was cold, as it has been for two days now, and we lighted a coal fire. In the afternoon we went for a two-and-a-half-hour walk – quite pleasant. It was muddy underfoot but fine, though rather overcast, and a comfortable temperature for walking (in thick coats). Not many people were out, apart from soldiers with their girls.

We did not bother to decorate elaborately, but Mrs. Turner [mother of a former school friend] gave us some of her variegated holly, which looks quite attractive in vases. People seem to have sent as many Christmas cards as ever; but the Minister of Supply has asked that they and all wrappings shall be put aside as salvage.

This morning – feeling festive! – we opened a bottle of home-made damson wine given us by Mrs. Turner two years ago. It was quite agreeable.

I had to go on duty at 2300.

Thursday 26 December Last night was the busiest night watch I've yet known.

One of the 'Mayor's' assistants (P.H.O. Jackson) came to lunch and tea. His wife is in hospital at the moment. We were talking about the time when I was with Roberts, and some of the odd things I came across. It is great fun looking back on it now; it is such a contrast with my present work. [E.A. Roberts was the free-lance journalist mentioned earlier. He had an extensive connection with trade papers, which entailed my attending such thrilling events as meetings of the Boot Repairers' Association, the Fish Friers' organization and an assortment of others, ranging from hairdressers to bakers – some in Plymouth, others in places such as Newton Abbot, Exeter or Torquay. Most were held in evenings, necessitating slow and often cold journeys by bus, eating a sandwich supper en route. Many of the meetings were excruciatingly dull, some quite interesting and a few downright bizarre – such as the meeting of about eight members who regularly produced an object like a miniature pig-trough, which was solemnly laid on the floor at the front of the meeting. Probably it was intended as an outsize ashtray, but I believed it to be a spittoon. It was never used as such – but the suspense was dreadful.]

There were no air raids by the Luftwaffe or the RAF at all on Christmas Day or today (including the night). The Italians bombed the open town of Corfu.

Friday 27 December Aerial activity was resumed today. . .

Lord Lothian[1], British Ambassador to USA, died some days ago and has been succeeded by Lord Halifax[2], the Foreign Secretary, whose place has been filled by Anthony Eden[3]. . .

The weather at the moment is very cold, but not so bad as it was last year, which was the most severe winter for very many years. It was pretty chilly going on duty by 0730 bus this morning.

Saturday 28 December Part of my uniform (jacket and one skirt) arrived today. I am very pleased with it.

In Plymouth this morning I met Mary and Mrs. Turner and Miss Kerle[4], – who turned on some of her usual stuff about 'My Girls'.

Monday 30 December On coming home to breakfast this morning, I found a chit from Mrs. Welby saying I had been promoted to 3rd Officer with seniority from 21 October. [The names of the WRNS 'rates' were the same as for the Navy – Wren, Leading Wren, Petty Officer, Chief Petty Officer – but the officers' ranks corresponded to those of the Merchant Service – Third Officer, Second Officer, First Officer, Chief Officer. Socially we were a mixture: there were probably as many 'gossip column' surnames, and even a few titles, among the ratings as among the officers, who also included many people with no claim to distinction. [In the afternoon I had the final fitting for my greatcoat, which should be ready some time this week.

It is now stated that Hitler asked Pétain[5] to permit transport of troops across unoccupied France for the use of the French fleet and for naval bases, to all of which demands Pétain sent a denial by Admiral Darlan[6], Minister of Marine. . .

London was heavily attacked, mainly with incendiary bombs, last night, and many churches and other valuable buildings were damaged or destroyed – among them Guildhall, which was gutted. St. Paul's was in danger at one time, but escaped serious damage. The *Daily Telegraph* did not

---

1. The 11th Marquis of Lothian (1882–1940).
2. 1st Earl of Halifax (1881–1959). Viceroy of India (as Baron Irwin) 1926–31. Foreign Secretary 1938–40.
3. Later 1st Earl of Avon (1897–1997). Foreign Secretary 1935–38 (resigned as protest against negotiations with Mussolini). Prime Minister 1955–56.
4. Miss W. Carlyon Kerle, formerly principal of my school.
5. Marshal Henri Philippe Pétain (1856–1951), a hero of the First World War, at 84 had become Prime Minister in 1940 after the defeat of France and established a government at Vichy, not then under German occupation.
6. Jean Francois Darlan (1881–1942). Commanded French Navy 1939–40; Vice Premier 1941–42. Assassinated 1942.

arrive until the evening but the *Daily Mail* was more or less on time. Just now the papers are showing advertisements of 'sales', which are apparently taking place as usual.

We were able to buy oranges again today, more plentifully than on Saturday, when I could only get four (one pound). Today eggs are down by 3d a dozen – to about 3/8d a dozen.

1941

CHAPTER I

Blitz on Plymouth

Plymouth

Wednesday 1 January I am starting a cold which is on its way round the office, so I didn't get up till 1400. I'm having Thursday, Friday and Saturday off, so I thought I ought to go on duty this evening. I didn't feel too fit.

Thursday 2 January I stayed in bed.

There was no meat to be had today, and it was announced that in future the ration is to be 1/6d a week (including pork and offals) instead of 1/10d excluding them. Cuts are also to be made in the Service rations of meat and sugar [for those not living in Service quarters] – which I think is a good thing. I know my allowances of those two things are considerably more than I eat.

Friday 3 January . . .Cardiff was heavily raided last night. . .

There was a slight fall of snow yesterday, and it continues very cold, though not so severe as last winter. Blizzards are reported right across Europe. About this time last year the Russo-Finnish war was being fought, in literally Arctic conditions; and hundreds of bodies were found frozen – in a sector where the Russians were being held. It was horrible to read about.

I think my cold must have been of the 'flu' type – it is still present and fairly heavy. I seem to have passed it on to Letitia, too.

Saturday 4 January . . .I was able to go out today, but have been told by the doctor I must take a week off, which is rather tiresome. It continues very cold, and the kitchen taps are frozen.

Sunday 5 January Letitia is now laid up with a cold, so I had to rally round and cook the lunch, consisting of boiled salmon with parsley sauce, potatoes, canned fruit and custard. It was edible. 'The Mayor' had to sleep in barracks; but on going in at mid-day, managed to get time off till dark. . .

Monday 6 January Bardia [Libya] has fallen, taken by Australians with the support of British tanks. It was bombarded from air, sea and land for thirty hours before the attack was launched. The whole operation took two days, and about 30,000 prisoners, with material, were taken . . . The German reaction is that it is quite an important success for us (very generous!) while at the same time the issue of a major war cannot be decided in Libya. [This entry has been given at length since it is typical of events in the North African campaign.]

   I have not heard from Terry for some days.

Tuesday 7 January . . . There were no air raids in this country last night, and the weather prevented RAF operations over Germany. . .

Wednesday 8 January . . . Baden Powell[1], founder of the Boy Scouts, has died. I think I should have put that in yesterday, but I get the dates mixed up.

   I returned to duty at 1800.

Friday 10 January My hat arrived today, so that I was able to appear in all my glory. Letitia persuaded me to go out in it this afternoon, but I felt rather too self-conscious to want to repeat the performance. However, I was very glad to get out of my rating's uniform.

Saturday 11 January Portsmouth was bombed last night. The Air Ministry said two bombers were shot down; but the German communiqué admitted the loss of six. It is the first time that this has happened!. . .

Monday 13 January This evening, while I was on duty, we had rather a blitz i.e. a blitzkrieg (used now to mean a heavy air raid). A good many fires were started, but they were all out by the time I came home. High explosives were dropped too, but I don't know to what extent damage was done.

Tuesday 14 January There is no electricity: we have gas, but other parts of the city have neither. We managed to buy a gas ring this morning and so

---

1. 1st Baron Baden-Powell (1857–1941).

were able to have a normal lunch, but there were no oil stoves to be had in Plymouth. Spooners and Dingles had only their provision departments open, and I think Pophams were shut. [These were all department stores in the city centre.] The telephone is working; but we can't get the BBC news because the wireless runs on the electric main. The raid lasted about three hours – I'm not sure because we [the office] were busy at the time. The lights went, of course, but by the time we had organized candles, the auxiliary plant was working and we had electric light again.

This morning the roads and pavements were covered with ice and very slippery; but it thawed later in the day and was quite pleasant this afternoon.

According to the *Evening Herald*, eighteen people were killed in the raid. [Later amended to 26, and about 120 injured. 106 high explosive bombs were dropped; 60 houses demolished and 400 seriously damaged[1]]

Wednesday 15 January From this morning we had electricity again; but I think part of Plymouth is still without, and also without gas . . . About 120 or 130 people were made homeless in the raid, in which about 10,000 incendiaries – not to mention HE's – were dropped. Portsmouth had a fire raid at the week-end in which 25,000 incendiaries were dropped. . .

This evening snow fell.

Terry has sustained slight concussion in a Rugger match (on Saturday).

Thursday 16 January It was extremely cold all day, and this afternoon it snowed quite heavily. . .

Yesterday I read T.S. Eliot's new poem, *East Coker*. I like the versification: it is so simple and direct. It will bear quite a lot of re-reading, I think. I have also been re-reading *Pilgrim's Progress*; but I get on much more slowly than when I first read it, at a very early age. I had to take to Macaulay's essays as a change.

Saturday 18 January This afternoon we went to a flick [film] – the first time I have been since Dunkirk. During the summer I didn't have time, and got out of the way of going – nor did I miss it. We saw *I Love You Again*, a so-called comedy (meaning farce), in which the leading players were William Powell and Myrna Loy, a spy-cum-detective film, a rather amusing 'short' about a kitten, and a newsreel showing scenes in Athens – among other things, a RAF man being carried shoulder-high through the

---

1. Twyford, p.110.

streets – and the naval bombardment of Bardia. Quite a good (light) programme lasting about three hours. We had very good seats – 2/6d, later 2/- (the top price).

When we were almost home, there was a single flash of lightning, followed by a heavy clap of thunder. Then we saw a peculiar red glow high in the sky, but not clearly visible, owing to thick cloud. After a few seconds burning fragments of something began to appear – one of the barrage balloons had been struck. Some children came running by, saying 'Flares!' – they did look almost as if they were. One of the pieces landed in the road, still burning; and I half expected someone to dash out and extinguish it with sand or a stirrup-pump. Everybody keeps (or should) at least one bucket each of sand and water at hand, ready to deal with incendiary bombs. . .

A letter from Terry today, who seems to be progressing.

Tuesday 21 January . . .President Roosevelt was today inaugurated as President for a third term of office.

Wednesday 22 January . . .The Communist newspapers, *The Daily Worker* and *The Week*, have been suppressed. Though this may seem necessary, I am inclined to think it unwise. It will drive the movement underground and give it a legitimate grievance. Also it will remove a means of knowing the ideas of the Communist Party.

This afternoon we saw four German planes – shot down – on RAF lorries in the Guildhall Square.

Friday 24 January . . .There have been no air raids on this country for five nights, and only slight activity by day. Such a lull seems rather ominous. It is probably due to bad weather, though on one of the nights in question the RAF attacked Düsseldorf. . .

Marshal Pétain has set up a National Council to advise him. It is reported that many of the members have four or more children. This should make them excellent advisers.

Monday 27 January . . .There has recently been a severe spell of cold weather, almost comparable to the 'great freeze' about this time last year.

My uniform grant (£30) arrived today.

There have been some unexplained explosions of gas mains in several streets of Plymouth. The supply was to have been restored in part to-morrow, but this will delay it again.

Tuesday 28 January On the way home from duty, we had a puncture – as we did going on at 2300 on Sunday. [We = members of 'A' watch. At that time we travelled to and from Egg Buckland Keep by van or a lorry with a canvas tilt and seats along the sides.] We had resigned ourselves to waiting while the wheel was changed, when the C in C's car (empty) came along and his chauffeur offered us a lift. Needless to say, we accepted; it was a great improvement on the usual van! On Sunday the [Wren] driver had to change a wheel in the dark, assisted by a policeman and a special constable. Or rather by the latter; the bobby lent a torch but didn't do anything more active. And next morning three of us missed the van going home because 'B' watch was late taking over; and just by chance, we managed to scrounge a duty car containing a stray naval officer. . .

Thursday 30 January . . .London was attacked last night, though on a small scale. . .

The Lease and Lend Bill, which proposes to lend material to this country, repayable in kind after the War, has passed the US Foreign Affairs Committee.

This morning, in a fit of energy, I stripped the dining-room windows of their anti-blast cellophane and paper strapping, which were going mouldy, and replaced them with net (ex-curtains) stuck to the glass. It is an improvement.

Sunday 2 February It snowed hard all this morning and part of the afternoon, and settled to a depth of about three inches. Then it thawed a bit and afterwards froze very hard. The roads were very difficult this evening, covered with a slippery uneven coating of ice and snow.

Wednesday 5 February . . .Very cold, with heavy rain and a strong wind. Most of the snow has gone, but some remains in odd corners and it seems almost colder than before. . .

Air raids on this country were on a larger scale than for the past fortnight. It has been stated by an RAF senior officer that the lull was entirely attributable to the weather. . .

Friday 7 February . . .This afternoon Letitia and I went to see Chaplin's *The Great Dictator*. It was rather better than I had expected – in fact it was good. There is practically no attempt to disguise the fact that it is aimed at Germany and Italy.

Wednesday 12 February Admiral Darlan has been appointed Foreign Minister. . .

Saturday 15 February . . .The night before last we had our nearest bomb yet. About 0315 I heard an aeroplane go over and after a pause it seemed to come back. I heard a pretty loud bang and decided it might be a good idea to go downstairs. While I was putting on my air-raid clothes, I heard an even louder rushing sound, almost like the propeller of an aeroplane rotating with the engine off, and lay down on the floor. There was a really heavy explosion and my curtains billowed out into the room. I thought the windows had gone, and lay there waiting for the ceiling to come down; but it didn't. We had no damage, but one window and one door were blown open. After a little while we put on coats and tin hats and went out. It hadn't dropped in this road, but quite a lot of windows nearby were broken. When I went out at 0730 to go on duty I met a Wren Petty Officer, who told me her ceiling had fallen in while she was in bed. She was unhurt. (11 people were killed in the Ford district, across the valley[1])

Sunday 23 February . . .For three nights – Wednesday, Thursday and Friday – Swansea has been heavily bombed.

To turn to smaller matters – at the end of the week we made some marmalade. Seville oranges had been promised for some time, and we had almost begun to give up hope of them. The sugar we were able to collect without difficulty, because none of us have it in tea. The butter ration is shortly to be doubled, making it 4 ounces per head each week.

Terry is doubtfully supposed to be coming home on leave to-morrow.

Sunday 2 March Terry arrived on Wednesday – which explains the gap in these entries. I was lucky enough to get Thursday night off.

During the week Bulgaria has signed a pact with the Axis. . .

Ex-King Alfonso of Spain has died, in Rome.

British troops have occupied Mogadishu, the capital of Italian Somaliland. . .

The new American Ambassador (Winant[2]) has arrived in England and was welcomed by the King.

Monday 3 March Today Terry and I went for a walk on the moor –

1. Twyford p.111.
2. John Gilbert Winant (1889–1947); Ambassador 1941–46.

Yelverton to Peak Hill. It was very pleasant. Except for a few showers, it was sunny and quite warm. We took lunch with us and came home in time for tea.

Tuesday 4 March This morning I had my hair cut short again. It cost me 7/6d, with wash and set, but I was pleased with the way they did it. In the afternoon we went to a flick, *He Stayed for Breakfast*. Quite amusing. It seems to me that America must be very nervous of Communism to make so many pictures holding it up to ridicule, cf. Ninotchka.

Wednesday 5 March Terry went back today, by the Cornish Riviera Express, leaving here at 1230 and reaching London at 1730. He ought to be in Chesham [Bucks] by 1914. . .

Having been given (by swap) Monday night off and by changing a 0800–1630 watch for 1630–2300, today I was able to have Monday and Tuesday with Terry and also see him off this morning. His seven days have gone very quickly.

Saturday 8 March . . .In an interview, the C. in C. HF (Admiral Tovey[1]) has said he is sure we can beat invasion if and when it comes. It is a subject that occurs a good deal in speeches now. There are various theories about the means by which it may be attempted – by troop and tank-carrying barges, self-propelled or otherwise, troop-carrying aircraft, possibly towing trains of gliders, and of course parachutists in various disguises, who would presumably be landed as saboteurs and raiders.

I am going to put in for leave from 21 to 28 March; we hope to go and stay at Chesham, if Terry can find a place for us.

Tuesday 11 March The Lease and Lend Bill has been passed by Congress and has been signed by President Roosevelt. . .

Terry is now Staff Sergeant again [having for some now forgotten reason temporarily lost the acting rank].

Monday 17 March . . .We have both had our seven days' leave approved, and [my parents and I] go to Chartridge, near Chesham, on Friday. Terry has found digs for us on a farm.

Thursday 20 March The King and Queen visited Plymouth today. 'The

---

1. Commander in Chief, Home Fleet: Admiral Sir John (later Lord) Tovey, GCB, KBE, DSO.

Mayor' was one of the few presented at the Royal Marine Barracks. I did not see them myself.

This evening we had rather a blitz, from 2030 to 01– something. The sky to the south was lit up with a red glow, which we heard later was Spooner's shop. There was a good deal of gunfire. We heard that the Royal Hotel, the Gaumont Cinema and the London Furnishing Company's shop had all gone – but of course it may not all be true. [The main attack was on the centre of the city, consisting mostly of shops and offices, and much of the damage was by fire, or the casualties would have been heavier[1]. At the time we did not know how severe the raid had really been, because full details were not given at once. Otherwise we should probably not have gone away as we did.]

Friday 21 March This morning we left for Chartridge. On reaching North Road Station, we found it in a bit of a mess. One platform had been hit and a train burned out. There was a dead man on the [station] roof. After we had waited some time, I asked if the train was ever coming and was told that there was a time-bomb on the line which prevented up and down traffic from passing through. Our train was due at 0832, but we had to wait for two hours in frost and fog, getting very cold. Men were working to clear up the mess, and after a little while they were joined by a RN working party. There were hundreds of people waiting, mostly Service. Eventually a down train came in, and as it could not go on any further, they took off a bit of it and by some miracle got everybody in. We left at 1030, at a snail's pace and stopping at literally every station. It took two hours to get to Newton Abbot. There was no restaurant car, and we had to go into different compartments. Fortunately we were travelling first class (free warrants).

At Newton there was a string of carriages waiting to be joined on to a London train, and we all made a wild rush. Our original one was to go via Bristol, and would have taken ages to get anywhere. However, we now had a restaurant car (and very good lunch and tea) and went through Westbury, stopping only at Exeter. We reached Paddington at 1730, on time, got a connection at Baker Street at 1810 and finally arrived at Chesham about 1920. I had sent a wire (by proxy) from Exeter to tell Terry we should be about three hours late, but he did not get it and so spent the evening calling at the station. We fetched up at last, however, and took a taxi to Chartridge.

---

1. Twyford pp. 114–5. See entry for 22nd March.

Saturday 22 March Plymouth had another heavy raid last night, said to be worse then the previous night's one. [It was, again, mainly on the central area, and most of the damage was caused by fire. 336 civilians were killed in the two raids.] Terry tried to ring his parents, but could not get through. Mrs. Pond, who is staying at Wendover, about six miles away, while Cyril[1] is away, came over this afternoon. We were conducted round the farm, which is fruit, vegetable and dairy, with a herd of fine Jersey cows.

Monday 24 March Went by bus to Windsor, where we had lunch and tea with relations. Some of the Eton boats were out on the river.

The King was apparently in residence at the Castle.

In the evening we saw *The Thief of Baghdad* at Chesham.

Wednesday 26 March Terry was able to get 48 hours' leave (today and to-morrow) and we [he and I alone for once] had a wonderful day. We walked to Great Missenden, where we had lunch at the Tapping House – somewhat given to quaintery – during an alert (the only one during our leave). There is no cinema at Missenden, so we took the first bus available to the first place of any size, which happened to be Aylesbury. There we saw a rather good film, *Neutral Port*, and had tea in a funny little cafe in the square where the buses stop. We had very thick margarine and paste sandwiches and rather good lemon curd tarts. By this time it was raining hard. We took a bus back to Missenden, not knowing whether there was a connection or not, but were lucky enough to get one immediately. It was one of the most delightful days I've had.

Thursday 27 March This morning Terry and I walked to New Amersham and back ... The wireless was on in the cafe and we heard the one o'clock news: there has been a revolution in Jugoslavia in protest against the agreement with Germany. King Peter, supported by the Army and apparently most of the people, has taken over, five months before coming of age. Winston Churchill has promised help...

In the evening Terry and I walked down to the farther meadows behind the house. It was a lovely evening, very still and clear, and the birds were singing. Bird song here is wonderful. It is gentle rolling country, with pale short grass and pale flinty soil and scattered beech woods: the villages with many old houses, red-tiled, and timbered, the walls a soft old yellow and the red of the roofs subdued by weathering.

---

1. Lieutenant (later Major) C.A. Pond R.M.

George Street, Plymouth, after the bombing. (Photograph by The Western Morning News.)

It has been a delightful holiday – too quickly past, of course – and very peaceful. But Devonshire spoils one for 'soft' country.

One sad thing happened – the sapphire has come out of my ring and I cannot wear it. A jeweller in Windsor replaced it but would not say it was secure, and I am afraid of losing it. Till I can have it re-set, I shall wear the turquoise one [formerly my father's mother's – a group of turquoises round a small ruby.]

Friday 28 March [by 0842 train from Chesham, arriving back at Plymouth at 1530]. Last week's raid on Plymouth was severe. All the centre of the city has apparently gone – Bedford Street, Old Town Street, Guildhall Square, George Street, Westwell Street and part of Union Street, in addition to sporadic damage in other parts. The buses stop short at York Street, Plymouth, and Manor Street, Stonehouse: the part beyond is roped off on account of unexploded bombs and blasting of dangerous buildings. One time-bomb which exploded yesterday killed the Bomb Disposal Squad at work on it.

Our house is untouched. The chief question is how shall we get food. Dingle's, where we had registered [under rationing regulations] is gone – in the course of the destruction Berenice [who was Secretary of the company] did marvels with the others in trying to save the building – and so of course is the original Food Office. [Mutley Plain now became the main shopping centre for the 'Plymouth' end of the city: the original shops found temporary accommodation in small premises – private houses or whatever could be obtained. The 'Devonport' end was still intact at this stage[1].

Terry had a letter to say that the office of [the solicitor to whom he had been articled] is destroyed. Over the week-end he tried to telephone home, but the exchange would take only urgent calls. In the end he sent a wire and his father rang up on Monday morning.

We walked up to Blockhouse to get a view of the town, but it was too wet and misty to see much. St. Andrew's church tower still stands; but the ribs of the Guildhall were sticking up bare, and there seemed to be a good few dents and blanks in the skyline. However, there's quite a lot left yet, apart from the business area.

Monday 31 March . . . This afternoon I went out in a Women's Voluntary Service mobile canteen (a converted single-deck bus). Starting from

---

1. Twyford p.115.

Greenbank Police Station, we went down North Hill into (I think) Looe Street, where we stopped to hand out tea and sandwiches to the soldiers working on the ruins – and anybody else who asked. While we were there, a gang of soldiers hauled down a section of dangerous wall. It fell about twenty yards away with a heavy crash. Civilians were carrying cases and bundles of salvaged things away from (their) damaged houses. An old man asked if he might have a cup of tea and 'anything to bite', and said he was 'so grateful'. Our next stop was in Woolster Street, which had suffered a good deal of damage, and then we went on to what I afterwards discovered was Treville Street – at first I though it was St. Andrew Street, which leads (or led) from St. Andrew's Church to Notte Street. It was quite unrecognizable. The shops were piles of broken stone, and the steel girders inside were twisted and bent. The air was full of dust, swirling by now and then in thick grey clouds. The soldiers were covered with it and were working in their anti-gas eyeshades. For about half an hour we were handing out tea as fast as we could, to officers and soldiers of every description, plus sailors, RAF men and police. We finished up in Old Town Street, by Spooners', which is a most extraordinary sight. The building has ceased to exist, except for a segment where some other shops jutted into it. There is literally nothing but a very low pile of rubbish, and the supporting girders, which are twisted and contorted. Some, still perpendicular, have drooped at the top like dead flowers. An alert sounded while we were there, but nobody took any notice, or even hurried.

The people are wonderful. On the lorries helping people to move are written tags: 'RN and RAF Co. Ltd. Estimates free. Anything anywhere. We move, like Beechams': and the bonnets are decorated with Union Jacks, artificial flowers and paper festoons and bells. Some servicemen gave us a huge bunch of daffodils, produced from inside their lorry, and another gave us a little cheap vase from somewhere as a souvenir. I was amused by one North Country soldier, who found time to comment on the weather: 'You read about sunny Devon at school, but I haven't seen much sun here in six months.' Most of the area where we went was closed to the public and under military control, though there were a few stray boys, whom the soldiers shooed off. A girl, not too intelligent by her looks, came up pushing an old pram and asked for some tea. She said she had been given a pass to go and fetch four chairs and a tea-set from her bombed home. She was delighted. In another place we saw women standing by a house while soldiers passed them out some of their belongings. One woman was holding a frying pan and a rubber hot water bottle.

I was told of a WRNS rating who arrived home after the blitz and found the rest of the family of nine had been killed, and who yet thought to ring up and say that she did not feel up to going on duty on the next watch.

The German cruisers *Scharnhorst* and *Gneisenau*, which have lately been attacking merchant shipping in the Western Atlantic, are known to be at Brest. They were bombed by the RAF last night, but though they were straddled, no direct hit was observed...

Tuesday 1 April Losses of merchant shipping for the week ended March 23/4 were 59,141 tons (24,940 British) ...Weekly averages, taken over periods of a month, have been: July 84,000, August 86,000, September 103,000, October 86,000, November 86,000, December 70,000, January 55,000, February 74,000 March (first three weeks) 84,000.

Casualties in two raids on Clydeside on 13 and 14 March amounted to 1,100 killed and 1,000 seriously injured.

...During the past financial year, national expenditure was £3,867,000,000 – or about £10,500,000 a day, £3,220,000,000 of it being war expenditure – and revenue £1,409,000,000.

After tea we walked to, or rather round, Plymouth – down Molesworth Road, round the bottom of the Hoe to the Barbican. The Hoe proper is still closed; and while we were walking along Madeira Road, a police car came by, announcing: 'An unexploded bomb will pass along here in a few minutes. Take cover.' We went into the concrete gallery above the bathing pool.

I saw for the first time what remains of George Street, Millbay and Union Street. George Street is just a heap of rubble and Westwell Street little better. One of the most amazing things is to look across what was a block of buildings and see something about a quarter of a mile away. One can do that from St. Andrew's Cross and Princess Square, along George Street, where the only shops standing are Dunn's and Page Keen and Page. Many of the shops have re-opened in premises disused, or given up to them, by other firms. Buses are running fairly normally, though of course they have to make a detour round the centre of the city.

Thursday 3 April The death of Virginia Woolf[1] is presumed: she has been missing for some days and is thought to have fallen in to the river Ouse (Sussex)...

Sunday 6 April Germany has declared war on, and already attacked,

---

1. The novelist (1882–1941).

Jugoslavia and Greece. British (or rather Imperial) troops have entered Addis Ababa (capital of Abyssinia)...

Monday 7 April Budget Day. Income tax is to be increased to 10s in the £, and the highest scale of surtax to 19/6d. Tax will be payable on incomes of £110 [per annum], and allowances will be reduced; but the amounts paid on account of the latter measure will be credited to the taxpayer as 'savings' repayable after the War. There are no increases in indirect taxation.

Thursday 10 April Eleven German aircraft were brought down last night, making the total for the past three nights 27.

US is to give us ten revenue cutters, which are described as fast well-armed vessels of nearly 2,000 tons.

Friday 11 April Good Friday – but is being used as a working day, except by the majority of the shops. It feels queer, not quite normal and not a holiday; there aren't even any hot cross buns.

Easter Sunday 13 April I had rather a strenuous day, coming off at 8 a.m., I had to go on with 'C' watch at 1600, because three of their people are ill. In a way it was rather fun, because I ran the watch; I am to stay there for the next few days.

Wednesday 16 April ...Unified resistance in Jugoslavia is now at an end, but it is expected that guerrilla warfare will continue.

Thursday 17 April ...London last night suffered the heaviest raid of the War. No further details have been published.

This morning we put down [i.e. preserved in waterglass] 4 dozen eggs, the Ministry of Food having announced that there will be no further decrease in price. They cost 2/6d a dozen: we hope to add to them next week. From 5 May cheese is to be rationed – 2 ounces a week per head. Jam, marmalade and syrup have for some weeks been rationed to a total of half a pound a month.

Sunday 20 April ...London had another heavy raid last night. In the Wednesday night raid St. Paul's was hit again and many other churches.

CHAPTER II

Bombed Out

Monday 21 to 28 April During the past week Plymouth – or more especially Devonport – has been subjected to a genuine blitz. [The local government unit of Plymouth had been formed by the amalgamation of Plymouth, Devonport and Stonehouse, and the identities of the 'Three Towns' remained in people's minds, so that they would talk about going to Plymouth or Devonport, for example.]

On Monday last we went to Torquay for the day and had a marvellous time. The shops and town are undamaged; it would be hard to know there is a war on. For tea we had sweet cakes, better than any we have had since the War started. The town is full of people, and of money, judging by the prices charged in the shops – 5/- a pound for tomatoes, for instance. So many people had gone over from Plymouth for the day that two special buses were needed to get them all back.

About 9.30 p.m. the sirens went and the raid continued until about 4 in the morning. Bombs fell very near to us, at the back and further along the lane [between the back gardens of the houses – a Plymouth speciality.] Several times we heard not only the whistling as they fell, but also the explosion and a rattling crash as if the entire top of the house had fallen in. But it had not – the only damage was a few holes in the roof. The people next door had their glass conservatory smashed, and came into us. There were some fires, but not very near. We managed to get some of the roof patched next day [by the emergency services], but not all of it. A house was demolished about thirty yards away, and another had a bomb in the garden.

At the same time on Tuesday another raid started – worse than the previous one. A house in the road was hit, and one that had a bomb behind it on Monday had one in front. The whole side of Ford Workhouse facing us across the valley went up in flames. It was an amazing sight – a mass of flame. After a little, one could see molten lead dripping down, and could hear the rush of the flames and the crash of beams falling in. There was another fire on the top of Ford [district], several in Stoke and others further off.

I was at home on both these evenings, but on Wednesday I was on duty when the raid began, once again at the same time. I do not think it was quite as heavy as the other two; perhaps that was because being on duty, I felt better. We weren't relieved until about 0230, when we had to come by a devious route owing to unexploded bombs and blocked roads. A big fire [oil storage tanks] was burning in the direction of Torpoint: every now and then the flames leapt up and illuminated the whole sky. It went on burning till at least the third day after the raid, showing a dense column of black smoke by day and a glow of fire by night. There were two or three unexploded bombs in the road, or just off it, so it was closed to traffic, and some houses were evacuated. We were within the rope [marking the dangerous area], but not near enough to the bomb to have to go. We had front windows broken but otherwise no damage.

The following night I should have gone on duty at 2300. I waited half an hour at the corner, which was open, but no van came. So I left a message with the Home Guard on duty, after vainly trying to telephone, and went home, where I sat up till 1245 and then went to bed.

Edna Deacon was killed on 21 April. [She was an air-raid warden]. Owing to an unexploded bomb, the rest of the family are at Plymstock and Higher Compton. Shirley and Warick [youngest sister, and brother – correctly so spelt] came home. We rather expected Terry but he did not come. Communications have not been very good.

In the series of raids, Plymouth as well as Devonport was damaged, particularly in the region of Drake Circus, which had escaped before. Dingle's lost seven of their temporary shops, leaving only two. Fore Street, Devonport, is said no longer to exist. Stonehouse was also hit to some extent. Casualties were considerable (no figures). [Once again there was serious damage by fire in the central part of the city, as well as destruction by high explosive bombs – much of the latter at the Devonport end, among naval and military establishments and neighbouring districts. Service casualties were not announced in total, but a direct hit on the petty officers' block in the RN Barracks killed about eighty. Seventy-two people were killed in a public underground shelter in the central area of the city[1].]

Today (28th) one of our bombs was dug up and its fuse removed, so the road was re-opened in the afternoon. We saw the bomb after it had been operated on. It was a small one, about three or four feet long. One in Mannamead exploded and killed three Bomb Disposal Squad soldiers.

1. Twyford p.120.

Service working parties have been out clearing roads and demolishing dangerous buildings. Many people go out of the town each night to sleep: some have been taken out in buses. I think it is a bad thing, liable to lead to nervous exhaustion and panic. Some homeless people have been living in shelters. We are very lucky, having water and electricity, though no gas, and have done some cooking for neighbours.

This morning I took some clothing down to the WVS clothing depot and stayed to help distribute. During the lunch hour I collected some more from neighbours and ourselves; and we scrounged a lift in a van to get it there. It is rather pathetic, some of the people are so apologetic and grateful. Others are quite fussy. In any case it is awful to see them dressed up in odd bits and pieces – all they have been able to save – they are covered, not clad. Some very attractive gifts were sent by American children, containing things for children of various ages, all classified and done up in gay print bags.

This evening there was a fairly heavy raid from about 9.45 to 0100 [resulting in damage on the Devonport side and adjacent villages in East Cornwall.[1]] There were some fires, but it was not as bad as the others. My van came for me before the all-clear, but did not know the road was open, so I had to stand outside and look for it. Bombs dropped fairly near again and broke a window at the back.

Tuesday 29 April ...War Zone Courts have been constituted. They will not function in any area until it has been declared a war zone, when they will operate with wide powers.

Two planes were brought down in each of two raids on Plymouth, and another four last night...

Plymouth is now to be an evacuation area. For the past fifteen months the C-in-C and the Lord Mayor have been trying to get it scheduled. It is now said to be one of the worst blitzed places in the country.

Wednesday 30 April Last night we had a very heavy raid, lasting from just before 10 until about 0200. We were in a way prepared, because when we went out after tea to call on Mrs. Deacon – who we found is staying at Plymstock for a bit – there was an alert, which is often a fore-runner of a night raid. My father was on [fire] watch in RMB from the afternoon until next mid-day; so I spent a little while consciously screwing up my courage (if any). I haven't felt particularly brave since we have had bombs

1. Twyford p.124.

so near; when I hear them whistling down, I find myself shaking, and it is very hard to control.

We were listening to the news when, at about 9.15 p.m., it faded out – a sign that enemy aircraft are about – so we got our things together and changed into air-raid clothes. Nothing happened for half an hour; and we had just decided it was a false alarm when the siren came. As usual the [family from next door] came in for shelter.

I thought we had had heavy raids, but I have never heard anything like this. The A/A barrage was very loud, and all the bombs seemed to be within hearing distance. We could hear first the planes, then the guns, bombs falling and then exploding – knowing what was coming and waiting for it. This went on for what seemed a very long time, with one or two bombs coming especially near. Then there was one explosion far greater than any of the others. The house shook and seemed to move forward, the doors burst open and the remaining windows fell out. Lying on the floor, I confidently expected the house to fall in on us – but nothing came, in spite of crashes which we found later were made by wardrobes and so on falling down on the floor. I got up and saw that it was light, with a yellow glare. From the dining-room door I could see a spout of flame coming from one of the gas-holders [down in the valley], and a house in the terrace immediately behind us burning fiercely. The floor was littered with small objects and debris, but I kicked it back and managed to shut the door. We had to turn the light off in the refuge, because the doors were gone [in front, and the light would have showed], and sit in the dark. [The little girl from next door] was very brave, but I had to get whisky for the others and lime juice. I was worried lest sparks from the burning house at the back might blow into the open dining-room: but the Auxiliary Fire Service were working on it, for we saw the reflected glow on the drawing-room wall fade and die out in about ten minutes. The gas holder soon stopped burning. We sat in the dark, having gone back after a first attempt to rush out, which was silly. [The neighbours from the other side] looked into see if we were safe and then went to shelter at Milehouse – but I thought it was much better to stay put.

Towards the end of the raid they began to drop 'Land mines'. We knew this because there was no whistling, but a flash, followed by a heavy explosion. It was a very long time to us before the all-clear sounded.

We found the house was standing, but badly damaged. The window frames were wrenched bodily out, and the sliding doors [between front and back downstairs rooms – another Plymouth speciality in smaller houses – from their frame. Upstairs seemed to be much worse – in the dark, quite hopeless, but later we found that though the roof at the back was just about gone, and the plaster off the walls and ceilings, the floors were sound and it was possible to get about. Water and electricity remained, so we made tea for our party and [other neighbours], and I took the surplus to the firemen who were finishing off the burning house. We cleared up a bit and then lay down to rest in the refuge. None of us slept, and about 5.30 I got up and dressed. We had breakfast and then I walked to the RM Barracks [probably two or three miles, to tell my father we were still alive – which by that time he had decided was unlikely – and to see what help could be obtained.] Stoke was a mess. I was supposed to go on duty at 0800, but rang up to explain why I could not. We were able to get a lorry for the afternoon, and friends [who asked for their name to be omitted] offered to put us up for a day or two in their flat at Plympton. In the afternoon the Service lorry took us and a lot of our more portable belongings out there. It was by then too late for me to go on duty, which worried me, because other people in the watch had turned up after being bombed.

[In the five nights of bombing during April, 590 civilians were killed; many others were reported missing and were never found. 1,144 were injured. In the series of raids during March and April the number of houses destroyed or damaged (including some several times) was 72,102. 24 churches of all denominations were destroyed. 'By this time the heart of Plymouth had been gutted, and Devonport had been similarly treated. It was a fearful sight. The main shopping streets of Old Town Street, Bedford Street, George Street, Frankfort Street, Cornwall Street, Treville Street, a considerable portion of Union Street, Courtenay Street, Fore Street (Devonport), Marlborough Street, Tavistock Street, Catherine Street, St. Aubyn Street, and many other side and back streets adjacent to them were virtually wiped out of existence, and there were scores of other places like Princess Square, Westwell Street, Lockyer Street, Athenaeum Street, Millbay Road, and whole areas of private houses in the Hoe District, at Keyham, Ford, Swilly, Beacon Park, and other parts of the city completely destroyed ... 'There was not a single part of the city which escaped, either business or residential, and there was scarcely a house in the entire area which did not sustain some damage, either serious or minor'[1].

Between June 1940 and April 1944 Plymouth had a total of 602 alerts; on 59 of them bombs were dropped. Casualties were (civilians only: Service figures were not given):-

---

1. Twyford, pp 98 and 125 and passim.

killed	1,172
seriously injured	1,092
slightly injured	2,177
missing, believed killed	7
	4,448]

1–3 May On Thursday I slept at the fort after duty and on Friday went in by bicycle. This I did again on Sunday evening. It was easier than bus, but fairly strenuous. Thousands of people had transferred themselves to Plympton, travelling to and fro by bus, car, lorry, cattle truck or anything on wheels, and some walking. It was pathetic to see them straggling out in the evening. Some slept in railway 'door-to-door' containers.

Four of 'A' watch – Phil[1] and Zélie[2], Mrs. Dent and I, were bombed out. Phil and Zélie were injured. [They did not return to the watch, but were posted to Dartsmouth.]

Monday 5 May 'Midsummer Time' [i.e. with the clocks advanced two hours from Greenwich Mean Time] started on Sunday. On Monday we moved into the Bracken's house [at Mannamead, Plymouth. They were the parents of a former schoolfellow – now Mrs. Joan Hillis]. They were going to Pensilva for the summer. We had the lorry again, and a bigger one a day or two later to bring furniture. We were able to save nearly everything, though it was all very dirty and a good deal of it damaged. It is in a state of complete chaos, having been so hastily packed and put together.

Saturday 8 May A year ago the German army attacked Holland. . .

Air raids during the past week have been principally on Clydeside and Merseyside, and also on the North East. Plymouth has had warnings lasting from 2300 to 0500, which have spoilt one's sleep but did not develop into attacks. 20 bombers were brought down on one of these nights.

Sunday 11 May London was heavily bombed last night. 33 German aircraft were destroyed, 31 of them by night fighters. . .

Monday 12 May Rudolf Hess, Deputy Führer, has disappeared. The German version is that although on account of some disease Hitler had forbidden him to fly, he got hold of an aeroplane and is presumed dead.

1. Third (later Second) Officer Phillida Coode.
2. Third (later Second) Officer Zélie Llewellyn.

His adjutants have been arrested for connivance at his disobedience. It is also said that he was suffering from hallucinations and is more or less insane – though a week or two ago he was making speeches in public.

Tuesday 13 May Hess has been found in Scotland, where he landed by parachute after flying from Augsburg. According to doctors he is quite sane and healthy, though slightly injured. There are a good many theories about his arrival: that it is an elaborate ruse on the part of the Nazis: that he came to prime prisoners of war with details of the plans for invasion, and that it was a routine visit to secret agents that went wrong. His plane was a Messerschmitt 100, which has not sufficient range to make the return journey. German propaganda now suggests that he may have thought he could bring about peace, but he had no proposals with him. He brought compressed food and photographs to prove his identity; and was captured by a Scottish crofter. [After being held as a prisoner of war, Hess was tried as a war criminal and sentenced to imprisonment at Spandau, where he still is (aged 87) at the time of writing.]

Here in Mannamead it is almost like living in the country. We have birds singing all day and coming down for scraps. They are mostly thrushes and blackbirds, with occasional blue tits. The cat next door (Mrs. Simpson) wears a bell so as to warn them.

Thursday 15 May On asking at the Gas Company's office today, I found that the supply was restored on Monday. We had apparently missed the Company's man sent round to announce it. Up to now we have been cooking on an electric 'ring', supplemented by the dining-room fire, and using the copper to heat water.

[The house we were in was Victorian, substantially built, with old-fashioned kitchen and scullery, with equipment, such as the 'copper' for boiling clothes, to match. When I showed these pages to Mrs. Hillis, her comment was: 'I had forgotten all about the copper and can't remember if my mother used it to get hot water when we were without gas [after previous raids]. I remember her cooking on the dining-room fire in a large black iron saucepan. I think we lived on mutton stews for about a fortnight, until the gas came back. I remember the copper being used when I was a small child. We had a washerwoman (Mrs. Clemo – I even remember the name), who came on Mondays to do the washing and the whole of the kitchen part was filled with steam.' She also recalls hitting the dog, Dash, over the head with the copper stick and receiving similar treatment from her mother in retaliation – but at the other end. [A copper-stick was about three feet long and two inches in diameter, needed to lift the clothes out of the boiling water.]

On the way to [our old house] (principally to collect some pet plants) I heard some of the most terrible talk I have yet listened to. It was a woman who admitted that she felt bitter, saying that 'that Hess' had come over for safety (!), to save his own skin and so on. She said she would hand him over to the Chief Rabbi: and that she would like to 'pull out his tongue a yard long and cut it off'. As for loving a German, she would not mind being shot down so long as she could have the satisfaction of inflicting pain on him. And a good deal more to the same effect. It made me feel depressed. It is dreadful that people should feel like that. One can understand it if they have suffered; but how are we to build a new world if people think of each other in that way? It will be very hard after this War to control the blind desire for revenge in order to work out some fairly rational and enduring settlement.

The destruction and damage one sees are sad but they are, even so, only incidents, illustrations of the far greater tragedy that two of the greatest nations should devote all their energies to exterminating each other, dragging the world with them. And this in its turn is an illustration of the state of humanity – not to see the folly and futility of such a war, to sacrifice their people and goods for nothing at all, or at best territorial aggrandisement on the one side. We say we fight for civilization; so we do, for civilization as we know it – not that it will ever be the same again; but we did not realize it two years ago as we do now. A good many people still do not really comprehend the fact.

Friday 16 May . . .The damage to our house (or the cost of repair at 1938 prices, as required for the war damage claim) has been assessed at £380. The roof needs reconstructing entirely. One of the inner walls has moved bodily two inches from its original position – apparently without damage.

Thursday 22 May . . .For the first time since the last blitz, I went to Plymouth today. More still has gone now.

Prices ruling at the moment are – lettuces 5d, tomatoes 5s a pound, spring onions (about 5) 5d or 6d, cucumbers 1/8d (you can buy half a cucumber for 10d). There were more cakes about than for some time. Food is quite plentiful; in fact we have not had difficulty in getting things.

Terry is coming home on leave in the first week of June.

Saturday 24 May HMS *Hood* has been lost. She met the *Bismarck* and other

German ships in Denmark Strait and was blown up by a hit in her magazine. *Bismarck* is damaged and is being pursued.

Sunday 25 May I went to Mattins at Emmanuel Church. There they have rented pews, which is a bad system. I was also irritated by catching sight of the hymn 'Sons of labour'; For condescending complacency it takes any prize. It is things like that that make people jeer at the Church of England.

Tuesday 27 May I woke up this afternoon after a strenuous and very thrilling night watch and heard that *Bismarck* had been sunk (by *Dorsetshire*) some hundred miles west of Brest. The *Prince of Wales*, which was present when *Hood* went down, engaged *Bismarck* and hit her next day. Later she was hit by torpedo-bombing aircraft from *Ark Royal* and *Victorious*, and by the time the pursuing ships caught up, was un-manoeuvrable, though able to fight. More than 100 ships were in the chase, including *King George V* (C. in C. Home Fleet) and *Cossack*, which seems to be in every action, *Norfolk*, and *Suffolk*, which did most of the shadowing. For a time *Bismarck* was lost; but was picked up again by the Coastal Command aircraft. She was alone, the *Prinz Eugen*, which was with her in Denmark Strait, having parted company. Admiral Lutjens sent a signal to Hitler saying that though incapable of manoeuvre, he would fight to the last shell; and went down with colours flying. . .

Wednesday 28 May The fighting in Crete is intense. The Germans have penetrated our defence in one place and both sides have been reinforced . . . All the operations are being carried out under intensive dive-bombing: I have the greatest admiration for the soldiers and sailors standing up to it.

President Roosevelt, in his 'Fireside Chat', has declared a state of 'Unlimited Emergency', under which the US will place her forces in 'strategical positions' and in every way make herself ready. It is explained that America will not convoy ships to Britain, but will devise some 'more efficient' method. In my opinion America will be in the War in a very short time. . .

Sunday 1 June We are withdrawing from Crete after violent fighting that has caused 'severe casualties', according to the communiqués, to both sides. About 15,000 troops have been taken off and landed in Egypt. . .

Clothes are to be rationed, starting at once. We shall have 66 coupons a year, which can be spent in any shop on any garment. A pair of stockings takes 2 coupons, pyjamas 8, a woollen dress 11, and cloth by the yard will take more or less, according to width.

Sir Hugh Walpole[1] has died, at the age of 57.

It was about this time last year that the evacuation of Dunkirk took place. The weather today was the same, fine and warm with a clear sky. Last year it was hot, but it didn't seem to hinder anyone from working hard. My hours at that time went up from 9 to 5 to 9 to 8 and never again went below 9 to 7. Some of the French troops [70,000 to 80,000] passed through Plymouth on their way back to France. I remember being held up on my way home by bicycle to let a column of them pass. They were laden with rolled-up blankets and all kinds of gear, and walked with the rolling step of men carrying heavy weights. They were tired and dirty, but seemed pretty cheerful, making the 'Thumbs up' sign as they went by. There were all kinds of races mixed up. I noticed one Chinese walking along with a completely detached expression. The best-looking were the Moorish contingent, who held themselves well and looked proud.

Thursday 5 June The ex-Kaiser has died at Doorn, where he lived after his abdication in 1918.

Monday 9 June to Thursday 11 . . .Terry came home for seven days' leave on Monday. I managed to get seven days' leave at the same time.

On Thursday 'the Mayor' was sent to RN Hospital for his septic arm, started at the time of the last blitz. (Came out next day because it wasn't necessary to operate. He had his arm in a frame for several days, and has been given three weeks' sick leave.)

Monday 16 June Terry went back today. The seven days passed very quickly. We had two days on the moor. On the first we walked from Tavistock to Cox Tor and back through Peter Tavy, and on the second walked from Wrangaton up Ugborough Beacon (Eastern) to Three Barrows and back down the Western Beacon to Bittaford. It was wonderful. On Saturday we saw the film *Quiet Wedding*.

On Monday afternoon I bought a hat (18/11d, which, though more than I wanted to pay, I suppose isn't too bad, including purchase tax.)

. . .It was a year ago on Sunday that France fell. I had an even more strenuous time than after Dunkirk. The Sound was full of ships; and with the full moon, we expected raids, but none came until the evacuation was

---

1. The novelist (1884–1941).

finished. Devonport in the evenings was swarming with all kinds of sailors and soldiers – Dutch, French, Polish, Belgian, Czech, Canadian, and of course hundreds of our own soldiers. . .

Tuesday 17 June I made a mistake about the fall of France. The date of the actual capitulation was 17 June; 15 was the day Marshal Pétain succeeded Reynaud[1].

[The first indication that something was amiss came on 14 June, when a division of the Canadian Army was to sail from Plymouth for France. After all the arrangements had been made and the troopships had actually left the Sound, the news – not public at that stage – came to the Naval Offices that they were on the way back. The reason was, of course, that French resistance had collapsed.

Several French warships made their way to Plymouth, among them the old battleship *Paris*, which served as a depot ship for a short time. At the beginning of July, in view of the uncertain relationship between the French and German Governments, it was decided that the French ships should be seized, in case they sailed to join the German navy. They were accordingly surrounded by British ships, and armed boarding parties took over. The Commander in Chief (Admiral Sir Martin Dunbar-Nasmith VC) went in person to receive the surrender of the French Admiral – unarmed, since only a little while before, the Admiral had been a guest in his house. In the course of the operation one man on each side was killed, in another ship[2].

Later, *Paris*, which would not have been fit for use as a fighting vessel, was allowed to sail for France, but was torpedoed in the Channel by a German submarine. The crew was rescued, including a very friendly young lieutenant whom many of us knew. He came back looking for sympathy among his WRNS acquaintances, who, far from regarding him as an unfortunate hero, told him in no uncertain terms that it served him right for trying to go back.]

The price of gooseberries is to be 5d a pound. Up to now it has been about 1/2d. Today we were able to get enough for jam.

Thursday 19 June Turkey has signed a non-aggression pact with Germany. I was not very much surprised, because their attitude has been rather more aloof all the War than one would expect from an ally. . .

1. Paul Reynaud (1878–1966) Prime Minister March–June 1940: as President, Pétain succeeded Albert Lebrun (1871–1950).
2. Twyford chapter IX passim for dates and supplementary details.

Saturday 21 June Shipping losses for May were over 400,000 tons – 98 ships – which is less than for April. . .

There are rumours about German–Russian disagreement and the massing of German troops on the frontier. I should think they are likely to be wishful thinking, or German propaganda. The general opinion is that Germany will not attack Russia just yet.

Sunday 22 June Germany is at war with Russia 'to save Europe from Bolshevism'. A proclamation by Hitler, read by Goebbels[1] at 5.30 a.m., accused USSR of having failed to fulfil the terms of the non-aggression pact signed in August 1939 and of sabotage in Germany. Molotov has denounced the attack as unprovoked aggression. Finland and Rumania are said to be helping Germany. There have already been air raids on Kaunas, Kiev and Sebastopol. This seems to justify Russia's actions in annexing Lithuania, Estonia, Latvia and Bessarabia – and almost the Finnish War – and to support her explanations at the time that they were measures of protection against invasion . . . Winston Churchill is to broadcast this evening. (He promised help to Russia, which was later accepted.)

Wednesday 25 June Russia claims to have inflicted on the Germans heavy casualties in men and tanks, and to have destroyed 381 aircraft, losing 374 herself. Both sides have carried out air raids. The Germans claim to have taken Brest Litovsk . . . During daylight 'offensive sweeps' carried out over Northern France in the past ten days, the RAF have bombed power plants and railways and shot down 136 aircraft for the loss of 37. The price of gooseberries is now controlled at 5d; gooseberries, like most things when price is controlled, have apparently disappeared. Tomatoes are now 1/4½d a pound (controlled) and strawberries are to be controlled next week.

Monday 30 June Paderewski[2] died, in America, today. . .

---

1. Paul Josef Goebbels (1897–1945) Minister of Propaganda from 1933.
2. Ignacz Jean Paderewski (1860–1941) pianist; Prime Minister of Poland during 1919.

CHAPTER III

A Change of House

July 8–11 ...We moved on Wednesday 8th, to Compton Park Villas Road, a very pleasant house. [This was rented by my parents for the remainder of the War and a few years afterwards.]

Sunday 13 July We have signed an agreement with Russia, to come into force at once, by which each will help the other and neither will conclude a separate peace without consultation. This brought up the vexed question of the national anthems played before the 9 o'clock news on Sundays: would the BBC play the Internationale? They got out of it, more or less gracefully, by playing 'a favourite Russian march'. Later in the week it was announced that the anthems [of all the allied nations] are to be scrapped in favour of short concerts of national music...

Wednesday 16 July ...There are curious rumours, emanating from Russia, that Hitler has had a difference of opinion on the conduct of the War with Goering[1] and more or less deposed him from the command of the Luftwaffe.

After duty this afternoon, Betty Bayne[2], Pauline[3] and I went to see *Major Barbara* (the film).

Sunday 20 July ...The 'V' campaign started today in earnest. The object is apparently to encourage people in occupied territories to write V for Victory on walls and to tap out V in Morse [...] and so on. They have even brought in the Fifth Symphony [Beethoven], which starts with this V morse rhythm. My private opinion is that it is rather childish, like a schoolboy secret society; but I may be wrong. I hope so; but unless something comes of it it seems pointless...

Monday 21 July Having volunteered as a donor under the RN Blood Transfusion scheme, I was called up this morning to go to RNB. It was

---

1. Marshal Hermann Wilhelm Goering (1893–1946).
2. Third Officer: Mrs. R Bayne.
3. Third Officer: Miss P.M. Penn.

quite painless apart from a prick and a curious tingling sensation in my arm. I felt a bit wuzzy towards the end, but after the regulation rest and cups of sweet tea, I was perfectly all right.

Thursday 24 July The Russo-German fighting is still violent in some sectors, but the front is so vast that it is difficult to form a picture. . .

. . .Terry has been moved to Essex – Layer de la Haye.

Eggs are now rationed at the rate of two a week.

Out of 2,000 Marines who went to Crete, 1,100 were lost or left behind . . . We heard from Mrs. Pond yesterday, saying that Cyril was apparently not in the Crete Brigade and is safe.

Our old house is being repaired by the Corporation. They appear to be making a very good job of it, rebuilding the roof completely, in fact doing it far better even than we had hoped.

Friday 25 July Yesterday in daylight the RAF carried out the biggest 'offensive sweep' of the War, directed principally at Brest . . . 33 German fighters were shot down: we lost 15 bombers and 12 fighters. Direct hits were made on the *Gneisenau* at Brest – 7 claimed – and on *Scharnhorst* at La Pallice, and *Prinz Eugen* at Brest was straddled. Damage was also done to the docks. We saw some of the aircraft on their way back.

Wednesday 30 July We have seen two quite good films during the week – *Victory*, based on the book by Conrad, and *The Prime Minister*, with John Gielgud in the part of Disraeli. The dialogue fell down occasionally – Mrs. Wyndham Lewis: 'Really you are horrid', and the Chartist agitator: 'Spare the rich and soak the poor'.

Thursday 31 July I have been lent a magazine published by the de Gaulle French, *La France Libre*. This issue contains some very good articles – the best I have yet read about the War. . .

When I go on duty at 0730, I always see a cat sitting on the doorstep of a house opposite by a bus stop. [By this time we were working in purpose-built accommodation at Mount Wise, and were transported to and from it in an elderly open-top double-deck bus.] It waits there every day for an old man, presumably somebody's gardener, who picks it up and takes it along with him.

Friday 1 August . . .Poland and Russia have signed an agreement by which Russia denies the validity of the settlement made with Germany in 1939, by which she occupied Eastern Poland . . . An amnesty is to be granted to Poles imprisoned in Russia . . . and a Polish Army is to be raised in Russia.

Saturday 2 August Today we went to Lew Down to see Mrs. Turner, who is at Hayne. [Mary, my friend, seems not to have been there]. It is a Carolean house in pleasant grounds, used at the moment as a guest house. Both there and by the railway the wild flowers were wonderful, especially the willow-herb. We sat on a tree-trunk and watched the dragon-flies which were hovering over the water. There were trout in the stream. Between the house and the river there is a grotto with walls stuck with shells, which is said to have been designed by Horace Walpole. It is rather ruinous, which is a pity, though it is not particularly beautiful – the last place I should choose to sit in on a summer day. Far too cold and spidery for my taste.

I have come to the conclusion that I am not a good diarist, because I leave too much out – it is gossip that makes diaries interesting – some things on purpose and others by accident, and because I usually haven't time, or can't be bothered, to write it up every day. . .

A Russian estimate of German casualties, including wounded and prisoners, is a million and a half . . . It is curious how thrilled one is that the Russians are holding out. At the beginning of the War we should have been depressed by their having retreated as much as they have. But after France, Jugoslavia and so on, it is wonderful to see anyone standing up to a blitzkrieg for any length of time.

I went to a 'flick' last night with Betty Bayne and Pauline. USA have now got to the stage of making comic films about their army. I wonder how long it will take them to reach the point at which they make serious ones, with a hero admired for military qualities.

Sunday 10 August The Queen broadcast this evening to the women of America.

Mr Attlee[1], Deputy Prime Minister, announced this afternoon that Winston Churchill had met President Roosevelt at sea and that they had issued a joint declaration. We went to Elburton to see Mrs. Deacon this afternoon; the announcement was just coming through as we got out of the bus. . .

Friday 15 August Churchill and Roosevelt . . . accompanied by the First Sea Lord, the Chief of the Imperial General Staff, Deputy Chief of Air

1. Clement Richard Attlee (1883–1967), later 1st Earl Attlee. Prime Minister 1945–51.

Staff and their US equivalents, discussed supply and strategy . . . A three-power conference between USA, USSR and Britain has been suggested. . .

From 1 October milk is to be rationed. Eggs have been rationed for some weeks past, at a variable rate. On Thursday we were able to get enough plums (controlled price 6½d a pound) to make jam. Gilbert Medland [son of a school friend of my mother's] is missing 'as a result of enemy action at sea'.

Saturday 23 August . . .Russia has announced approximate figures of losses in the fighting up to now:

	Germany	Russia
aeroplanes	6,000	4,000
tanks	8,000	6,000
casualties	1½ to 2 million	7 million

Sunday 24 August Churchill broadcast this evening, mostly about the meeting with Roosevelt. It was, I thought, better than his last one or two speeches.

Monday 25 August British and Indian troops entered Iran from Iraq and from the sea . . . We have landed airborne troops to protect the personnel of the Anglo-Iranian Oil Company. . .

During the past week or so I have sown spinach, beetroot, early peas and onions. Today we bought a big marrow for a shilling, to make jam. We have not been able to get marmalade for one or two weeks past, though there is plenty of jam about – probably because so many people have been taking their preserve ration entirely in marmalade. . .

Wednesday 27 August We find we have a neighbour-but-one who is of Polish extraction. Next door, on the other side, they have a Czech maid. They also have an infant called – constantly – Roger. . .

This evening it was announced that Pierre Laval and Marcel Déat[1], another pro-German, have been shot and wounded. . .

Thursday 28 August Reports about Laval and Déat are conflicting. They are in hospital and are apparently severely wounded, though perhaps not seriously.

A new government has been formed in Iran, and has ordered resistance to British and Russian troops to cease. . .

---

1. Marcel Déat (1894–1945) Minister for Air 1936. Formed Rassemblement Nationale Populaire earlier in 1941.

There has been a great flutter during the past two days over the announcement that instead of being segregated in the bay [in the canteen], we are at liberty to eat at any table, among naval officers etc. Some people went down early to avoid encounters, some wouldn't go down at all. I went at a normal time and found that in effect we had merely changed one table for another. All this fuss arose out of some Quarters people saying that 'after all their work' etc. etc. they were tired of being 'ignored'. So what. (Later I scored top marks by having supper with the Chief of Staff and [another Staff Officer]).

Friday 29 August The Russians have evacuated Dnieperpetrovsk and blown up the great dam across the Dnieper which supplied power to factories on both sides of the river. It was considered one of the greatest engineering achievements of its kind. I don't know how they could bear to destroy it. . .

Saturday 30 August . . .This morning I went into all the shops I could, asking what they charged to make a tweed suit. Luscombe said from 7 guineas plus purchase tax, Hector Powe from 6¹/₂ plus purchase tax. I think the latter is indicated! Recovered my watch from Pophams, who had sent it to St. Austell [Cornwall] to be overhauled, taking about three weeks. That was the only way I could get it done: neither Pages nor Bowdens can do repairs again yet. 10s for clean, overhaul and new glass.

This afternoon we went out to Maristow for blackberries. We picked 5 pounds, for blackberry and apple jam. It was lovely there – warm, and the air wonderfully clear, and the heather beginning. There was a fair number of aircraft about (RAF). Came back about 5.30 and slept before going on at 2300.

Wednesday 3 September The War began two years ago today. The announcement that it had been declared was made in Parliament at 1100, and on the wireless at 1300, by Neville Chamberlain. It was Sunday.

During the previous week Terry and I had been going about together as much as we could. I remember on the last afternoon we went to see the film *Bengal Lancer*, he in uniform, expecting to be called up [as a member of the Territorial Army – Royal Army Medical Corps] and mobilization was announced on the six o'clock news when we got back to his house. He packed his kit and came home with me to say goodbye. I wept buckets, imagining that he was going to France immediately. But he only went as far as Millbay Drill Hall and came to see us several times again before he was sent to Gillingham in Dorset.

From 1 September, when the German army invaded Poland, we had been expecting a declaration of war, and people were beginning to ask why we were delaying, in view of our unconditional guarantee to Poland. There were pictures in the paper of people digging trenches in the streets of Warsaw. Everybody felt dreadful when we heard of the air raids and tank attacks in Poland: it was so much more ruthless than anyone had known before. It had been fairly clear ever since the march into Czechoslovakia [March 1939] that war could not be avoided, and when the Russo-German pact was signed [August 1939], it was obvious. One expected Italy and Japan to attack at once, but of course Mussolini waited until France was finished and Japan still alternately fulminating and climbing down. . .

I have ordered a jacket and skirt from a tailor called Dean, who says he will charge 5 guineas. He must be very bad, I should think!

The Wren office seem to have got my leave well muddled. They allege that I had 10 days in May, in addition to what I really had, so that according to them I have had 22 out of my 28 days this year. Lt. Cdr. Parsons[1] [RNVR – one of the Signal Officers] is taking it up.

Saturday 6 September A submarine, presumably German, has made a torpedo attack on the US destroyer *Greer*, which has been ordered to 'eliminate' it. . .

Monday 8 September Two US ships have been sunk, one by aircraft in the Red Sea and one in the Atlantic (I think). . .

My leave has been approved.

Tuesday 9 September We have made a naval and military raid on Spitzbergen, to wreck coal mines and destroy stocks of coal and oil. A number of Norwegians were brought back to this country. I must say it seems a pity – though I suppose inevitable – to destroy coal when we are short ourselves. Though now there apparently isn't going to be rationing this winter, after all. (Nor of milk, though we shall probably have to use dried and canned to help it out). . .

Wednesday 10 September This morning I went out to Crapstone to lunch with Betty Bayne, after a couple of hours' blackberrying. We picked a vast

---

1. Lieutenant Commander S.T.T. Parsons RNVR; later Commander.

amount, which she insisted on making me have. It is the third time I have been blackberrying and I've had about enough now. I hitch-hiked back from the Rock in a lorry, arriving home at 1545, to go on duty at 1700.

CHAPTER IV

Of Fleas and Other Things

Sunday 14 September . . .President Roosevelt [has] announced that in waters considered by the US necessary to their defence, their ships will attack any Axis ships they meet. This does not imply a declaration of war.

On Thursday 'the Mayor' and I went to see the film *Target for Tonight*, which tells the story of a bombing raid on Germany. [This was an official showing for RN and RM people.] It was, I think, very well done, with excellent photography. One of the most effective sequences, in my opinion, was that showing the 'hero' bomber sailing along like a ship, rising and falling over the clouds. It made one realize how fantastic the whole thing is. [At this time the word 'fantastic' still had the meaning of fantasy-like.] All the actors were RAF personnel. The US Navy is now to protect approaches to Iceland, including the waters off Greenland and Labrador.

We have been very much bothered just lately with fleas in the beds in our dormitory. [The system was that anyone would could be spared during the night watch could go and sleep for an hour or two.] I was badly bitten on both of the last two night watches. Complaints have been met with the answer that cat fleas don't bite human beings. (No one ever said they were cat fleas – though in all probability they do come from the cats, which sleep on the beds and are absolutely crawling.] So this morning I wrote a nice official letter for Betty Dent to sign, hoping that it will provoke a storm.

Monday 15 September Today, being the day before a night watch, we went to Okehampton. We found a very pleasant walk by the river and up on to the moor. It was delightful there, with a view for miles across country to the north. I wasn't going into the flea farm again, so I took two rugs with me and slept on the floor, using my gas-mask as a pillow. It was surprisingly comfortable, and I slept better than in the dormitory.

Thursday 18 September The Shah of Persia[1] has abdicated, and is being succeeded by the Crown Prince[2], who is apparently going to rule as a

1. Riza Shah Pahlevi; seized power 1921; was proclaimed Shah 1925.
2. Mohammed Riza Shah Pahlevi (1919–80); superseded by Revolutionary Government 1979.

constitutional monarch . . . British and Russian troops are marching on Tehran.

Friday 19 September The Aurora Borealis was seen last night, and was accompanied by magnetic storms which made it impossible to pick up Moscow radio (for the usual communiqué) and interfered with transatlantic cables. I saw it on my way home, without knowing what it was. There was a pale greenish glow in the north, and another in the west, with long fingers of light, rather like dim searchlights, across the zenith from east to west.

The official answer about the fleas is a suggestion that we should provide ourselves with cotton sleeping-bags. I shall continue to sleep on the floor or the shelf.

Monday 22 September . . .Three British fascists escaped from internment in the Isle of Man over the week-end and tried to get to Ireland in a small boat. They were re-captured and the other internees rioted when it was found that they were not to return but to go to prison. They stoned the guards and threw bottles. The guards were armed, but were not allowed to fire unless the internees tried to get out, which they didn't. One wonders what will happen after the War: whether they will be released at once, and what they will do. I shouldn't think anyone'd have much time for them after this War.

The Aurora was seen again on Saturday night. It's been such lovely weather. I do hope it lasts for my leave.

Friday 26 September Sherry party at Quarters yesterday. Terry was to have arrived today, but a wire arrived at lunch-time to say that his leave had been postponed till Monday. I managed to get my leave put back too.

Saturday 27 September I went with Pauline Penn to see *Pimpernel Smith*. At the beginning of the week I saw a better film, *Dangerous Moonlight* – about a Polish pianist who became an airman.

Monday 29 September Terry arrived this afternoon looking very fit. We had previously had his father to lunch, and Berenice [came] in later. They have to give up their house at Elburton, and wanted some assistance. They decided on a house in Rockingham Road, about fifty yards from us. Mrs. Deacon is coming to see it to-morrow.

Wednesday 1 October A fine day. [Terry and I] walked from Horrabridge to Walkhampton and Princetown, where we ate our lunch, and then back to Tavistock, where we had tea – nearly 13 miles. It was most enjoyable, though in the middle of the day it was quite cold.

Friday 3 October Yesterday we went to Elburton again; and today – marvellously fine and warm – we went for another walk. We started from Bedford Bridge and walked down the Walkham past Grenofen and Denham Bridge. Then we had to go inland – which meant a good deal of going back to avoid trespassing – and through Milton Combe to Lopwell. From there we walked to Roborough, which seemed a long way – just missing a bus home. However, we got one [further on]. We were both pretty tired.

Saturday 4 October We all went to a rather good film, *Rage in Heaven* – adapted by Christopher Isherwood from the novel by James Hilton.

Sunday 5 October We [Terry and I] went to Elburton for lunch and came home for tea – having invited Miss Bessie before we knew about Terry's postponement.

Monday 6 October Terry went back, after 7 days which have passed very quickly.
   The Cherry Orchard is being played at Exeter by the Old Vic. I wrote for tickets on Saturday, intending to go up for the matinée on Thursday.
   This afternoon I went over to our old house, which we are having re-decorated. It is looking better, and will look more so when it gets glass in the windows. . . . Terry gave me a copy of Damon Runyon's *More than Somewhat*.

Wednesday 8 October This morning Letitia bought me my birthday present – a length of rather super peach-coloured crepe to make underclothes (badly needed). It is a lovely colour.
   No news from Exeter, so it looks as if that has fallen flat. This afternoon we went over to the house again to do some cleaning up. We have had the walls and ceilings distempered, and are now waiting for a man to come and do the windows.

Thursday 9 October . . .End of my leave at 2300, worse luck. I've never felt so reluctant to go back. I went to the dentist this morning. Nothing to be done again. I think it's more than two years since I last had a tooth filled. A most depressing day. We went to see *Cottage to Let*, a spy film. It was rather good. I was very sorry *The Cherry Orchard* fell through, though. Today Letitia bought some kippered mackerel – a new one on us – also two pounds of our onion ration.

Tanks have been on show here today as part of the production campaign. I didn't see them because I couldn't be bothered to stand and wait. . .

I have bought a copy of *Bomber Command*, the Ministry of Information booklet about British bombing since the beginning of the War. It is very well printed, and illustrated with some striking photographs. Haven't yet begun to read it. There are so many books I must read. There never seems to be time for all the things I want to do.

We have been eating our own vegetables lately – cabbage, cauliflower, spinach and curly kale. The peas I put in for next Spring are in bloom already, which is a pity, I think.

Friday 10 October This afternoon we went to Crafthole [across the Tamar, about five miles into Cornwall] for tea with the Hoskin family[1]. I got up rather later than I should have done and as a result we missed the 3 o'clock bus. However, someone gave us a lift to Tregantle and we walked from there. Lois gave us several pounds of very good apples.

Sunday 12 October This morning we walked to Egg Buckland Church for the service, which was most extraordinary. I have never seen vestments like those the vicar wore – a sort of cope, over a surplice with straight sleeves, and a yellow square back and front just below the knees. In the middle of the Nicene Creed – it was Choral Communion – he suddenly disappeared, and a few minutes later came back by another door, minus cope, and went into the pulpit. The sidesmen fussed about with their bags – and all this time the creed was still going on.

Tuesday 14 October to 20 October . . .Mary Fox[2] has promised to teach me squash, which will be a good thing – I don't get enough exercise.

. . .Milk rationing has come into force, but has made no difference at all. It is not likely to do so until later, when it may be necessary to supplement the fresh milk supply with condensed and dried milk.

'The Mayor' gave me Day Lewis and L.A.G. Strong's anthology of modern verse.

1. Parents of a former schoolfellow, Lois (the late Mrs. H.A.L. Whittaker).
2. Third Officer K.M. Fox.

We have had a plebiscite in the cypher office on proposed new hours in order to get a long week-end once a month – and it looks as if we shall have to have them. There seem to be quite a few changes in the air. . .

Tuesday 21 October Official sherry party at the Superintendent's house. I've never seen so many admirals in one room – C. in C.[1], Admiral Superintendent [of the Dockyard], Commodores by the handful, and Admiral Somerville[2] of Force H. The Duke of Gloucester [brother of King George VI] was there, having just got back from Gibraltar. Can't say I was much impressed. I had quite a chat with Captain Lush, whom it was nice to see again, and with Mrs. Lush. As usual, I was quite horrified by the number of WRNS I don't know.

Wednesday 22 October Terry is putting £5 into the Fund [our joint savings] as my birthday present.

Sunday 26 October . . .In France two German officers have been shot, one at Nantes and the other at Bordeaux. Two batches of 80 'hostages' have been shot because no information has been given about the former, and a similar threat has been made in connection with the other. . .

   . . .In a news film yesterday the swearing-in or whatnot of the new Shah of Persia was shown – with the streets lined by British and Russian soldiers. Poor man – he must feel very small.

   The Market is being fitted out with concrete stands to take the place of shops – Woolworths etc. – and corrugated iron booths are going up in what used to be Drake Street.

Friday 21 November . . .The *Ark Royal* has been torpedoed by a U-boat, which was later sunk by a corvette. German propaganda claimed to have sunk her at the beginning of the War and on many later occasions – even going so far as to promote and decorate the man who was supposed to have done it . . . Canned foods are to be rationed from December 1 on a system of point values.

   Miss Bessie showed some of my things to L.A.G. Strong[3], who wrote me a long letter and made various suggestions. [These 'things' were short stories and poems. I had always had literary ambitions but found it very difficult to get started. Mr. Strong took a surprising amount of trouble,

---

1. Admiral of the Fleet Sir Charles Forbes DSO (1880–1960).
2. Admiral of the Fleet Sir James Somerville GBE, KCB, DSO (1882–1949).
3. Leonard Alfred George Strong, novelist (1886–1958).

writing several letters with suggestions for improving one of the stories. However, events took a different turn, and the literary intentions were shelved.] One [in verse] he said was excellent.

I have gone on learning squash and have bought a racket (25s.).

Our watchkeeping system has been changed – at first to a very bad scheme whereby we not infrequently had to do 1800–2300, 0800–1300, 2300–0800 and 1800–2300. A 'bought it' completely, having to do a very hard turn-round to start it off, and a hectic week-end, after which it was revised to a plan of Pauline Penn's devising. Under this, each watch gets a long week-end every month, but it isn't nearly so strenuous. Anyway, it's better than the ratings' new watchkeeping – they now do a 14-hour night 1800–0800! [The system for WRNS was based on a four-day cycle, with four separate teams (watches), but admitted of many variations and was changed from time to time on request.]

The Navy has now started marching in threes [like the Army], so we had to go to RNB and see how it was done. I have rarely been so bored.

Monday 24 November . . . We have at last succeeded in letting our old house. The tenants move in to-morrow.

Yesterday I broke a back tooth – or rather, a biggish bit just came off; I was most disconcerted. Sims [dentist] is in London and I can't have anything done about it till Thursday, which is very annoying – particularly as I purposely didn't go to bed after night watch. However, I stayed up and went to buy Christmas presents this morning. This afternoon I am doing a 'flick' with Betty [Dent or Bayne?], and going on duty at 1800. I shall probably be completely unconscious by about 2000!

Up to 6 December . . . Japanese emissaries are still having 'conversations' with US in Washington, but they don't seem to be getting much forrarder.

We have now declared war on Finland, Hungary and Rumania, having given them an ultimatum requiring withdrawal from the fighting against Russia.

I was able to have my tooth filled, or rather re-constructed, which was by way of being a major performance. An even greater one was having my protruding upper canine extracted; I've been getting up my courage for that for several years.

Sunday 7 December Japan has carried out air raids on Pearl Harbour (Hawaii), on two places in the Philippines, and on other American islands.

Monday 8 December America has declared war on Japan, followed by Canada, Nicaragua and Costa Rica. Japanese troops have landed or attempted to land in Thailand and Northern Malaya [now Malaysia], where British troops are fighting. [The Japanese] have seized the International Settlement at Shanghai, and attacked Hong Kong from the Chinese mainland.

After the air raids on American territory, the Japanese in Washington told the US representatives that it wasn't any good going on with the conversations. The raid on Pearl Harbour seems to have been pretty heavy. Churchill broadcast this evening.

Thursday 18 December . . . Thailand gave up fighting Japan after three days. The situation in Malaya doesn't look too good. [The Japanese] . . . have landed in the Philippines, and at two places in Sarawak. In Libya . . . a battle is in progress some miles west of Tobruk.

This morning I bicycled out to Leigham Manor [nursing/convalescent home for WRNS] to see Priscilla[1], who was taken there a week ago . . . She won't be coming back to the watch, worse luck . . . Betty Dent goes on leave on Saturday, and then to Greenwich [as an instructor], so until their reliefs arrive, I'm left with Mary [Fox], Elsie[2] and Pauline, plus the rating typist. Yesterday I had a farewell binge with Betty – a 'flick', *Underground*, which was very harrowing – followed by supper at Malcolm's (3/6d – good but very dear). It was the first time I'd been to an evening 'flick' (in winter) since the War! There were two alerts in the course of the evening, but no one took any notice. . .

---

1. Third Officer, later Second Officer: Miss F.P. Chase, MBE. Her arrival earlier in the year was the beginning of a friendship which has lasted until her death some years ago.
2. Third Officer, later Second Officer: Elsie Vaughan.

1942

CHAPTER I

Promotion

Plymouth

Monday 13 April A good many things have happened since the last time I made an entry. [The Japanese had taken Hong Kong, Singapore, Java and part of what is now Malaysia and were currently invading Burma. Bombs had been dropped on North Australia, Ceylon and the East coast of India; and two cruisers (*Dorsetshire* and *Cornwall*) and an aircraft carrier (*Hermes*) had been sunk off Ceylon. Sir Stafford Cripps'[1] mission to India to discuss proposals for self-government and Dominion status had failed to reach agreement. There had been attacks on Norway and on Occupied France – notably on St. Nazaire. Indignation had been aroused by the success of the German ships, *Gneisenau* and *Prinz Eugen* in escaping from Brest and sailing up channel, in daylight, to Kiel and Wilhelmshaven.]

Terry took his Law Society final last month. [His articles to a Plymouth solicitor had, of course, been interrupted, but since the associated studies had been based on local lectures, supplemented by a correspondence course with law tutors, he had managed to continue with the latter during his Army service.] He won't know the result till the 17th.

Betty [Dent] having gone, I've now (just) got my second stripe [i.e. promotion to Second Officer, in charge of the watch]. Mary Fox having gone to Portsmouth, her place has been taken by Audrey Sampson[2]. We

One night watch I lost the sapphire from my engagement ring. We swept the office and looked everywhere but couldn't find it. When I took the ring back to Bowdens, they sent it back to the makers, who of course replaced the stone free of charge. Which was very lucky, though of course it should never have come out. I then proceeded to lose my fountain pen.

We recently had a 'Warship Week' here, in competition with Portsmouth (whom we beat); we raised £1,400,000 odd, having aimed at £1,200,000 (= HMS *Adventure*). I went out selling savings certificates in an ambulance

---

1. Sir (Richard) Stafford Cripps (1889–1952); Chancellor of the Exchequer 1947–50.
2. Third (later Second) Officer; A.L. Sampson.

one afternoon: we ended up with £312, but that was beaten by somebody else the next morning only – ours was the whole day's takings.

I had to go to lunch with the C. in C. one day. It was very formal and dull. [The cypher officers were invited in turn to join a lunch party: in my case it was not exactly helped by the fact that I had been on duty the previous night, and unwisely decided to go to bed for the morning; I should have been much more awake if I had stayed up. During the morning I was called to the telephone: the Flag Lieutenant, to say that on no account must I arrive with my hat wet; since it was raining, I must take a taxi. Pondering this strange command afterwards, I decided that, unless it was for purely aesthetic reasons, it must have been because our tricorne hats – which unlike the other women's services we wore indoors on formal occasions – collected water in their turn-ups, resulting in a miniature deluge when the head was bent forward; so that the apparent solicitude was probably more for the polished mahogany table than anything else. Umbrellas, of course, were unthinkable with uniform.]

Captain Lush has gone to Gibraltar. Before he went he gave a lunch party at the Grand Hotel to celebrate his CB. It was very pleasant.

Thursday 23 April . . .I had a great excitement last week-end. On Saturday I was told I must report at WRNS headquarters on Tuesday for the Signal Course Selection Board and spent a frantic morning telephoning and generally making arrangements. I went up on Monday morning to do a bit of shopping in London, and then to New Malden. . .

On Tuesday morning I was to meet the other Plymouth candidate, Patricia Somers-Brown[1], under Big Ben, but she didn't turn up. However, she appeared at Great Smith Street, and we travelled back together. I was pleased to find that the selection was from a short list (13) who had been weeded out from the large number of volunteers. [This was the first time the appointment of WRNS officers as Signal Officers had been considered.] However, there were only 6 vacancies. The Board consisted of the Director, First Officer Murie[2], and the Commander of the Signal School. The interview lasted about five minutes and seemed to be completely futile if the object was to find out how much one knew. [It probably wasn't, since that would have been dealt with in the preliminary weeding process, presumably.] As usual at interviews, I had the feeling that they slightly disapproved of me and that I had given the wrong answers to the questions. We don't know when the results will be made known.

1. Second Officer; Miss P. Somers-Brown MBE.
2. First Officer E. Murie.

I get a great thrill out of London, especially the famous buildings and streets. There were a lot of people about, including all the Allied forces imaginable, not to mention Canadians, airborne troops, commando-men and so on. In Regent Street there were US naval uniforms on sale, and almost every other Serviceman had either a Canadian or American accent. It was really great fun seeing it all – the best look-round I've yet had in London.

On Friday we heard that Terry had passed his Final. I sent him a greetings telegram asking him to ring me up while on duty on Friday evening – which he did. I'm very glad he's passed.

Thursday evening (to go back a day again) we listened to a recording of the enthronement of Dr. Temple[1] as Archbishop of Canterbury. I think he is an excellent choice.

Friday 1 May RAF has recently bombed industrial and military targets in Germany and occupied countries . . . As declared reprisals, Germany has bombed Bath, Exeter and Norwich and is said to be compiling a list of historic towns [hence the expression 'Baedeker raids'] for similar treatment, which their Ministry of Propaganda has been pleased to call the 'British-German cultural war'. . .

Visit of the King and Queen. We were inspected at Mount Wise by the Queen, who then went up the Hamoaze [the Tamar-Lynher estuary, dividing Plymouth from east Cornwall] in a boat manned by Wrens. The King, instead of driving according to schedule, walked past us when he found us still there after she had gone. The parade consisted of Wrens, nurses, ATS[2] and WAAF[3] – mostly Wrens.

. . .Terry's name is to go up for a commission. I am glad he is being given a chance of one.

[date illegible] Invasion exercise today and to-morrow all over Plymouth, with incidents, i.e. fictitious bombs, gas etc. in the streets. We were warned to expect one, but it wasn't near us after all. 'C' and 'D' watches had to sleep in, but 'A' watch got off quite lightly. I was very much amused by a major who, in the course of making some enquiries, explained to us that the enemy weren't really the enemy – but only for the exercise!

. . .Churchill broadcast this evening – an optimistic speech.

Anti-typhoid inoculation re-done.

---

1. William Temple (1881–1944).
2. Auxiliary Territorial Service: precursor of the Women's Royal Army Corps.
3. Women's Auxiliary Air Force: now Women's Royal Air Force.

Sunday 31 May . . .Last night the RAF made the biggest raid carried out by anyone, by sending more than 1,000 bombers to attack Cologne. It must have been terrible. We lost 44 aircraft – not all from the Cologne raid – bombers and fighters attacked aerodromes – as a diversion.

I was very glad to hear that Priscilla is better and will be going back to duty (don't know when or where).

My arm is still very stiff from the second instalment of TAB inoculation, done on Friday, but less uncomfortable than at first.

[date illegible] . . .This afternoon I took Elsie to Burrator. It was very hot – a perfect day – and very pleasant. I have rarely been so hot.

Wednesday 10 June I spent a very interesting afternoon with Elsie at Staddon [radio] station. The elderly lieutenant in charge explained it all to us and showed as the transmitters – most impressive. He also passed on an exercise message by [morse] lamp for our benefit. We had the most enormous and extraordinary tea I've ever eaten; soup, followed by huge plates of salad surmounted by large helpings of fresh crab. Then sweet cakes! Fortunately we had the walk back to Hooe.

Thursday 11 June The Director being down for a day or two, and we ['A' watch] not being on duty when she visited the cypher office, we had to go down to RNB before going on night watch. It was by way of being quite a state occasion with C. in C., naval officers by the dozen and a good few RM officers, to watch the WRNS drill competition, which was won by the [Area Combined Headquarters i.e. Mount Wise] squad. I was presented to the Director, and had to take her to my watch and tell her who was who. Quite a thrill! Then we were rushed off by duty car in order not to be too late, [the previous watch] having stayed on for our benefit. During the evening the coders filled their silver cup [for the drill competition] with cider and brought it round for everyone to take a drink.

Friday 12 June An Anglo-Soviet alliance has just been signed in London, by Molotov and Anthony Eden. It provides for full collaboration during the War . . . and is to last for 20 years, terminable or extensible after that time. I think this is an excellent thing and should be very valuable in straightening things out after the War.

Tuesday 16 June This afternoon we [several cypher officers] went on a very enjoyable tour sightseeing in the Dockyard and then by Wren-manned boat out to Breakwater Fort. The main idea was to see the respective signal stations, but we were also shown the very interesting gunnery works. A fighter aircraft was diving at the fort all the time we were there. Then we went on to a party given by Captain Tenison (Army), who went on the tour and invited everybody who went. Very superior eats – crayfish and salad, strawberries and cream – and large quantities of alcohol. We were shown a real lemon! His home is in Eire, whence he appears to have brought some of this plenty. Having had rather a busy night, I had some difficulty in keeping awake, but it was quite good fun.

Heard today that Kenneth Jolliffe [a childhood friend at Gosport] was killed on June 3 when his plane crashed in Syria. He was 25.

Thursday 18 June . . . Today a letter arrived from Cyril Pond in reply to one posted last September. His was dated 20 March . . . He talks about parrots, honey-birds, coconuts, pine-apples and kapok trees, but of course doesn't say where he is. [It was the Maldive Islands.]

I spoke to Priscilla on the telephone today. She is working under the Assistant Secretary[1] and seems to like it. [In time, this appointment in the Commander in Chief's office was to lead to the preparation for the invasion of Normandy – see entry for 1 May 1944]

Churchill is in America again for conversations with Roosevelt. [probably 23 June]

. . . Exactly a year since Germany attacked Russia. . .

The loss of Tobruk (surrendered) with some thousands of troops . . . has been confirmed. News has been pretty bad during the past week: shipping losses serious, and all the Libyan retreat.

Listened tonight to the first performance in this country of the Leningrad symphony by Shostakovitch. It was written in Leningrad under siege conditions last year. I thought it was rather fine, though usually I cannot understand contemporary music.

We are beginning to pick early peas, and for some days have been digging roots of early potatoes as we need them.

Wednesday 24 June Terry's birthday.

The House of Commons is taking, I think justifiably, a very poor view of the way in which the current campaign in Libya is being conducted. I think that what has made such a bad impression is the fall of Tobruk after a day.

---

1. Lieutenant-Commander A. Tapper; later Captain (S) Tapper CBE.

Thursday 2 July ...The situation is being debated in Parliament on a motion of censure. While many of the complaints, e.g. communiqués worded too optimistically, and the issues of inferiority of design and quantity of material – are well-founded, it seems rather futile to engage in such a discussion at such a moment.

On Tuesday I went over a submarine as a member of an organized party at the invitation of the Commanding Officer. We were taken round by the Sub-Lieutenant. It was very interesting. We saw their 'success' flag – a Jolly Roger with bars to denote ships torpedoed, stars for gun actions and a ram's head to commemorate sinking a ship by ramming, and captured German and Italian flags.

[date illegible] ...The motion of censure on the Government was defeated by 475 votes to 25...

The people next door having just had a greenhouse built, someone else a few houses away very kindly informed the Ministry of Labour or what-not, suggesting that it was a waste of manpower. An inspector was sent to look, but when it was explained that the greenhouse was to be used for growing food, the complaint fell rather flat.

Thursday 16 July Went this afternoon to see *How Green was my Valley* – a very good film – with Ann Wippell[1] and Audrey Llewellyn[2] [Zélie's sister]. As they are both ratings, I thought it best to go in plain clothes. On Saturday Ann goes to Greenwich for OTC. In her place [as typist in 'A' watch] we get a more difficult character, a tough Canadian, very efficient and keen, and a graduate, but inclined to be aggressive and officious. The other day we had a show-down, in the course of which I explained that the typist wasn't expected to run the watch! Since when we have been so exquisitely polite to each other that it almost hurts.

Commander Knapp[3] has been promoted and will be going, and Parsons is going ... next month. We said good-bye to Audrey Sampson today – I'm sorry she's had to go.

Friday 17 July This evening I missed the RN bus, having left the house at 1725, and, thanks to the tender mercies of the Corporation [bus service], didn't arrive on duty till 1825. Elsie was ringing up Letitia when I walked

---

1. Later Third Officer E.E.A. Wippell.
2. Later Third Officer A. Llewellyn.
3. Later Captain A.M. Knapp.

in, hot, much blown about and in a very bad temper. Conversation at Derry's Clock while we waited for the bus conductress to re-appear. Workman to driver: 'Going to stay here all night, mate?' Driver: 'Can't bloody well help myself.' Workman: 'Go on. I'll take the fares.' Driver: 'You can bloody well do what you bloody well like. Got to wait for the maid.' [Normal Devonshire usage for 'girl'].

Sunday 19 July Letitia's birthday. [My father] and I gave her a brown leather handbag, which cost the appalling sum of £2.10s. Before the War one could have bought it for about 25s. Celebrated yesterday with a lobster supper (my first), followed by lurid nightmare. . .

Friday 24 July In Russia the situation is very serious in the south, where the Germans claim to be fighting within the defences of Rostov ... General Auchinleck[1] has started an attack in Libya, or rather Egypt, which has been successful, though the army has not advanced a great distance. It is a most extraordinary campaign, in the way the two armies advance and retire in turn. . .

Last night on the way home I slipped getting on to the bus and cut a short but fairly deep gash in my left shin. It was quite painful and also spoilt a stocking – very annoying, particularly as I did the same stupid thing to the other leg [years ago] and have still got a notch to show for it. Serrated shins.

Sweets and chocolate are to be rationed from Sunday, at the rate of 2 ounces a week. . .

Vaccination. There have been cases of smallpox at Glasgow, Swindon and London – one is not allowed to go there unless one has been vaccinated within three years. [This must have been a regulation for naval personnel.]

Position in Russia seems to be very serious. The Germans are a long way south of Rostov, and ... their double movement towards Stalingrad is progressing. Further north the Russians seem to be doing better.

There are a few Communist posters about, urging the start of a 'Second Front'. While we probably aren't ready for it yet, it seems to me that if we leave it too late, Russia will be paralysed and Germany will be able to strengthen the western defences, with the result that any landing would be extremely hazardous.

I started leave on Friday – six days plus week-end. Terry is coming on

---

1. Sir Claude John Eye Auchinleck (1884–1980); later Field-Marshal.

Monday for nine days. The weather is very unsettled and inclined to rain. I hope it will improve.

Did a pleasant walk from Horrabridge to Ingra Tor and back through Walkhampton.

1942

CHAPTER II

Wedding Plans

Tuesday 11 August Terry arrived at 0630, having travelled all night. He slept till 10, and after lunch we went to Polhawn [on the Cornish coast a few miles away].

Sunday 16 August Went back to duty after a very pleasant leave, during the course of which we arranged to get married on Terry's next long leave. This won't be for some months if he goes to OCTU[1], but it seems really too good to be true...

Tuesday 18 August The last day of Terry's leave. We had arranged to walk from King Tor to Mary Tavy, but it had rained so heavily that we changed it to Lydford to Tavistock. However, while we were in the train, it started to rain so heavily that we got out at Tavistock instead, intending to eat our packed lunch in shelter and then go to a cinema. We had lunch by the river; and it stopped raining – also the cinemas don't open till evening – so we decided to walk back across Plaster Down to Horrabridge. It was oppressively hot but very pleasant. By evening I was very sleepy, having been on duty last night.

In the small hours of this morning British and Canadian troops carried out a landing at Dieppe . . . [withdrawing] as planned after about nine hours. Casualties are said to have been heavy on both sides...

Friday 28 August As usual while on leave, I lost track of nearly everything, so I will give a rough summary of what has been happening. Winston Churchill has visited Moscow, Persia and the Middle East, going by bomber. In Russia, the Germans have advanced a long way into the Caucasus and are also near to Stalingrad...

Mrs. Jackson next door very kindly gave me five clothing coupons to

---
1. Officer Cadet Training Unit.

buy a pair of shoes. I bought a stout walking pair with thick rubber soles – there won't be any more – 39/6d, which is fairly cheap as things are now. I have also bought a shirt blouse (35/6d), which I was allowed to sign for, and a pair of sheepskin slippers (17/9d). I also intend to get some underclothes, seeing that I can't have any of the other things one would normally have on getting married. [WRNS officers had no coupons, but could sign the bill when buying certain types of garment, including underclothes. It was an unsatisfactory system, because some shops did not understand it and suspected one of trying to evade the regulations. Later coupons were issued. Wren Joyce Tapp (now Mrs. Sears) has described the system as it applied to ratings: 'On my call up I gave away many of my things, mostly to my sister, who was nursing. Then on my first posting after training I found myself still needing slacks, the odd blouse and jumper, non-uniform underwear ... No service girl's wardrobe at that time could amount to much more than could be carried in one suitcase, or, in our cabins, stowed in two drawers and perhaps twelve inches of rail in a hanging cupboard.

'Nevertheless, in a time when clothing was rationed, there had to be a means of maintaining uniform, keeping together some kind of minimal civilian wardrobe that would suffice for informal occasions and allow us to purchase some of the more personal items without breach of regulations.

'As far as uniform was concerned, the only free issue was that received on initial kitting-out: jacket, skirt, overcoat, rain-coat, two shirts, four collars, two pairs each of shoes and black woollen stockings, and two pairs of 'blackouts'. This was our name for the regulation knee-length navy knickers, which were mandatory on parades but not on other occasions. Otherwise we were expected to maintain our uniforms and any other clothing out of our pay. For the Ordinary Wren, the lowest rank, this was twenty-eight shillings a fortnight (one pound forty pence). For upkeep we were allowed to spend two pounds a year, based on the official scale of prices at the official 'Pusser's'[1] naval store. A new shirt, for instance, would be debited against our account at two and seven (slightly less than fifteen pence); stockings, knickers and bra at one and eleven. All money thus expended was recorded in our paybooks. If we wished to purchase from civilian sources, the sum was recorded and a voucher was issued which authorized the transaction. A recognized scale of values in clothing coupons applied to each item. A voucher for pyjamas, which was worth seven coupons, was a most popular item. Seven coupons was also the

---

1. Purser.

official rationed value of a dress, or three and a half yards of material with which to make one. We were allowed to wear cardigans in place of our jackets when working, but vouchers for these were known to be used to buy pullovers as presents for someone special. They could also be used to get ten ounces (about two hundred and fifty grams) of knitting wool. . .'

Everyone in the Navy has to have an X-ray taken of their lungs as a precaution against tuberculosis. I had mine done on Tuesday. They take details of age, height and weight (142 lb): whether or not one ever learns the result of the photograph, I don't know.

On Monday 24th we (WRNS officers) gave a dance at the Lecture Hall, which is the only surviving part of the Guildhall. It was a great success. Unfortunately it had to stop at 2300 because of some rule about the hall. (7/6d plus 3/- for one guest and 2/- thereafter).

Monday 31 August Today, instead of sleeping, I did some bottom-drawer shopping – underclothes and pyjamas. It was great fun but very exhausting: we had to go from shop to shop because they had only small stocks and the sizes seemed to be [difficult? The manuscript has been damaged at this point.] I spent a lot of money, as follows: pyjamas 2 pairs at £1.1.11d, one at £1.4s (incidentally both the same but at different shops), two pairs of camiknickers (not very good but the best I could find in my size) £1.5s each, two satin petticoats and pants about £1.10s.

Tuesday 1 September Tonight Brita[1] and I had a farewell party with Zélie, her sister Audrey, and Susan [not identifiable]. We saw *The First of the Few*, about Mitchell, the designer of the Spitfire (very good), then supper of steak and chips (3/6d – very good steak). Zélie goes back to Dartmouth on Saturday. [Dartmouth was, among other things, a base for small craft such as motor torpedo-boats and motor gun boats, which undertook various operations in the Channel, often encountering similar German vessels, which used to attack convoys, especially at night. Often in the morning, after a night engagement of this kind, which sometimes also involved larger ships, such as destroyers, one would see officers rescued from some naval vessel coming to report to the Commander in Chief – still in their duffel coats, bare-legged, with whatever clothing they had been able to save. It gave one some slight inkling of what these night engagements really meant.

In my first job, with Captain Lush, we had evolved a procedure for

---

1. Third (later Second) Officer Brita Lang.

dealing with survivors, who at that stage were often landed in very large numbers from ships sunk by U-boats. A number of people in the RN Barracks and elsewhere needed to be informed at once, so that the men could be kitted out with new clothes, given a meal and sent on leave, so the 'drill' involved making a dozen or so urgent telephone messages. Another aspect of this is described by Miss Phyllis Hansell, then a Wren Writer working in the WRNS Office in the Royal Naval Barracks, Devonport:-

'When I had been in the Service about six weeks [i.e. in the summer of 1942] . . . I was told to report to the Drill Shed immediately – no reason given. When I arrived there I found eight typing desks with typewriters on them stretched right across the shed. Only then were we told that hundreds of survivors would be coming in and would queue up in front of our desks and we were to take down on sheets of paper all their details. We did this from 10 a.m. until approximately 3 p.m. It was the most wonderful feeling to know that we were helping these men to get on survivors' leave, and by 5 p.m. every man jack had gone. Naturally we had been told that never were we to divulge what we had been doing . . .' [At this point two or three pages of the diary are illegible].

Terry is now a cadet and is going to pre-OCTU infantry training. [He had now come to the conclusion that the best way in which he could help to bring the war to an end was to serve in a combatant unit. Never one to do things by halves, he volunteered for Airborne Forces. This was about the time of the victory of El Alamein, with the Eighth Army led by General Montgomery[1], who had been appointed to that command in August. The combined British and US landings under General Eisenhower[2] in North Africa took place on 8 November.]

Friday 27 November I went up to Kent for the week-end to see Terry. After flaps and spasms about getting accommodation, he rang up last night to say that he had booked a room for me at Meopham, the next village to Wrotham. I went up after night watch, on the 0835, arriving at Meopham soon after 4 p.m. Very nice house and people very kind (10/6d a night, in a private house). Terry came in just before 8 and had supper with me. On Saturday morning I walked to Wrotham (4 miles); not such a pretty village as Meopham Green, which was rather sweet, built round a green, with a windmill and an oast-house.

1. Bernard Law Montgomery (1887–1976); later Field-Marshal Montgomery of Alamein.
2. Dwight David Eisenhower (1890–1969); in command in Africa and Sicily; later Supreme Commander of Allied Forces invading Normandy: President of USA 1952–60.

In the afternoon we went to Gravesend for a 'flick' and supper. Sunday morning we went by bus to Sevenoaks, where we had a very good lunch and then went for a walk in Knole Park, which I thought most delightful. Afterwards we had tea and went back to Meopham. A very happy day – in fact the whole week-end was most enjoyable. I left next morning at 0830 – not having been called, but waking up under my own steam at 0710! – and arrived at Plymouth punctually at 1530, going on duty at 1800. I met Joy[1] at Paddington and travelled down with her. She had, in the meantime, been home to West Hartlepool.

Thursday 3 December This morning Letitia rang me up on duty to read a wire from Terry saying he would probably come home on leave this evening. I made preliminary arrangements to get some leave, to be confirmed by telephone in the morning. This evening I had to ring up the Post Office to get the text of Terry's next wire, because it hadn't arrived by 1900, which is the latest time for delivery of telegrams. He was to arrive about 0145, so I got up at 2 to wait for him. He came at something past three, and didn't ring the bell [to avoid disturbing us], so that if he hadn't coughed while bedding himself down by the garage, he would have stayed out till morning. I heard him, however, so he came in and had some hot soup before going to bed.

We had a lovely leave – unable to think or talk about anything but getting married. We bought a 'fixing present' (to celebrate getting it fixed) – a silver sugar caster, rather sweet. He gave me a little ivory Chinaman, which is most fascinating. For my birthday present we chose a wooden fruit bowl. We didn't do anything very special – walks, 'flicks', shopping and so on, and on my part sewing on buttons etc. etc., but it was very pleasant. He went back on Thursday 10th at 2245 to Morecambe for his OCTU and I returned to duty on Friday morning.

...The Russians are attacking in several sectors and have relieved the pressure on Stalingrad...

Monday 14 December Rommel[2] has withdrawn from El Agheila after putting up only slight resistance and the Eighth Army is advancing on Tripolitania. I think we were prepared for a battle at Agheila. The advance comes as very good news.

Letter from Terry this morning. He had a very trying journey. The 2315

1. Third (later Second) Officer S.J. Hope, who had recently joined 'A' watch and, like Priscilla, was to become a lifelong friend.
2. Field Marshal Erwin Rommel (1891–1944).

was cancelled and the 2330 would have reached London too late for the connection he had planned to catch. At Bristol he had a slight fuss with the Rail Transport Officer, who first told him the train wouldn't link up in London, and then that it would, after Terry and [another cadet] had got out of the train. They got back, and by getting a taxi reached Euston in time for the 0830 and finally arrived at Morecambe on time. He says conditions are much better there than at Wrotham, where for a time he was living in a marquee – in very damp cold weather.

1943

Wedding

Plymouth

Sunday 3 January ...Christmas was very quiet, and as usual I was rather bored. No turkey – we had pork...

Admiral Darlan was assassinated about a week ago by a Frenchman, in his office in Algiers.

Sir William Beveridge[1] has published his report, which is a draft plan of social insurance to be considered by the Government. The proposed flat rate of benefit is £2 a week, with contributions of about 4/6d a week. The report has not yet been discussed, but I should think there is not much doubt that something on its lines will be introduced.

Friday 22 January ...The Russians are advancing in several sectors, and have also relieved the siege of Leningrad...

There was a daylight raid in London, with some casualties, the other day.

Last week I managed to get a copy of *The Fall of Paris* (Ilya Ehrenburg). I haven't yet finished reading it, but it seems to be good and very moving in some parts.

Recently we have had two free Service film-shows – *Coastal Command*, a factual record of Coastal and RN work, and Noel Coward's *In Which We Serve*, which was more of a film in the ordinary sense of the word, and extremely good.

Saturday 23 January It was a very fine morning, with clear blue sky and quite warm sun. For about an hour there were bombers going over, singly and well up. Presumably some connection with the fact that American Fortress aircraft attacked Lorient and Brest today. Up to now it has been a mild winter. The daffodils are up about 6 inches, and polyanthus and auriculas are already in bloom.

---

1. William Henry Beveridge (1879–1963); later first Baron Beveridge.

Saturday 30 January Today the RAF, using Mosquito aircraft, made the first daylight raid on Berlin, or rather two raids. They were timed to interfere with speeches by Goering and Goebbels in celebration of the 19th anniversary of the Nazi Party's rise to power. . .

Most extraordinary weather. Coming off duty at 0800 I saw a balloon struck by lightning. More thunder and lightning later in the day, and a gale, but still quite mild.

Whipple's Comet, recently discovered, is now visible to the naked eye. I have not seen it yet, because the sky was not clear enough.

Woman's Journal wrote today offering 10/6d for one use of a poem 'When the Train Goes'[1] (Accepted).

Yesterday I and two others had the very dull job of auditing the WRNS officers' quarters accounts. However, there was a compensation – I learned that from 1 February we are to be allowed to sign for sports clothes (including skirts, jackets, stockings etc.) to the value of 21 coupons. I hope to get a suede jacket, if there are still any to be had.

Monday 1 February Peculiar weather continues, with wind and violent hailstorms. When I went on duty at 0730, there was also thunder and lightning. I got very wet walking to the bus, but managed to borrow a pair of stockings and went without my shoes in the office until they had dried. Hope I don't start a cold.

. . .The Russians . . . have captured F/M Paulus[2] at Stalingrad, where many of the German troops have surrendered, and the civilians are beginning to come back to what remains of the town. . .

Terry hopes to be here for a few days next week.

Saturday 6 January [should be February] All German resistance at Stalingrad has come to an end, and the Sixth Army has ceased to exist, having been killed or captured. Three days' mourning were decreed in Germany last week for the loss of this army, which their commentators regard as one of the greatest disasters that has ever happened to the German Army . . .

Sunday 7 February . . .Two daylight air raid warnings today, which the cats found most alarming. [This was our own cat, a former stray named Oliver, and his Siamese friend from next door.]

This evening I spent some time sewing the second of a pair of chamois

---

1. Reproduced on page 95.
2. Field Marshal Friedrich Paulus (1890–1957).

leather gloves I am making (chamois leather being unrationed). I suppose it's worth the trouble to get the gloves, but it's a fiddling job. I am also knitting Terry a pair of socks. In fact I seem to have a lot of odd jobs hanging over me – I want to make a frock and jersey, in addition to buying a new uniform hat, gloves, shirt etc.

I have been trying to get a copy of *War and Peace* – but it is impossible. Even Foyle's could not cope, so I had to get Underhill's to put my name down for a copy of the new 12/6d edition when it is re-printed in May. I had also ordered a book on Freud, just published – but it is alleged to be 'out of stock'.

Monday 8 February I had an egg today – the second within about four weeks, after almost three months without. Dried egg is quite good, but not the same.

Tuesday 9 February Terry arrived at 0220. I had to go on duty at 0800 until 1300, and again to-morrow night; after that I am having three days' leave.

Wednesday 10 February Terry went to the Vicar [The Revd. John Morris of Emmanuel Church, Mannamead], to put up the banns, after I had gone on duty. We seem to be spending most of the time in talking about the arrangements.

On Friday Terry had a long talk with Mr. Morris about marriage, and again on Saturday. On Sunday we went to morning service and heard the banns called. It was a curious feeling. Afterwards met the Vicar.

Terry went back by the 0845 train on Monday. Letitia and I went with him as far as Newton Abbot and then went by bus to Torquay, where we did some shopping. Met Pat[1] and Joy, by accident. After much trouble I at last managed to get a coat to go with my skirt, but it isn't as good as I should like it to be.

Friday 19 February This evening I went to see Mr. Morris about the service and so on. Rather a shattering conversation. [These interviews were at his invitation: he was very conscientious about preparing couples for marriage.]

Saturday 20 February This morning I had my eyes tested in the Barracks, having for some little while found that [they] got tired rather easily. It

---

1. Third (later Second) Officer Patricia Ommanney; Mrs. P. Neve.

seems I have got astigmatism in my right eye. I had to go in again about it on Monday afternoon.

It has been a Spring-like day; and we walked this afternoon from Crownhill to Plym Bridge and Plympton, which was very pleasant. Celandine, wild strawberries and periwinkles are in flower, and daffodils in the garden at home.

My fountain pen, having given out, has had to be sent away for repairs – estimated to take six weeks.

Monday 22 February The ophthalmic specialist seemed to be rather more optimistic about my eyes today – he said that if it were not for close work, I should not need glasses. However, he gave me a prescription for glasses but left it to me to decide whether or not to get it made up.

Tuesday 23 February This evening went to the Anglo-Polish Ballet (The first time I have seen ballet!). They did *Lac Des Cygnes*, various oddments, and *Cracow Wedding*. We enjoyed it very much and hope to go again before the week is out.

Had an egg for my lunch.

Tuesday 29 March . . .Winston Churchill . . . has broadcast on post-war planning – Beveridge Plan, plus four-year plan of general re-construction. . .

Four of us went up to Barnstaple for Joy Hole's[1] wedding on 8 March. Quite good fun – particularly on the return journey, on which we were joined by the clergyman uncle who conducted the service. At Yeoford we had to wait, so we went to the local pub, which wouldn't give us any food but let us sit in the bar and eat our sandwiches.

I have had a few wedding presents – a canteen of cutlery from The Mayor and Letitia, £10.10s from Warick, a tea set (white Utility but very nice), tea-spoons, Pyrex dishes and a very pretty set of fruit plates and dishes. ['Utility' was a standard applied to many kinds of goods, including clothes, to ensure that materials were not wasted in the production of luxurious articles. On the whole they were well designed and soundly made.]

My leave (compassionate!) starts on 6 April: 10 days, but joins on to a week-end which makes it a fortnight. [The point about compassionate leave, which was offered to me unasked, was that it did not count against

---

1. Third Officer.

the annual allocation.] I'm having a new suit of uniform to be married in. Everything is organized – Goodbody's are doing the catering (buffet) and after much hunting, we have managed to collect six bottles of sherry. Hymn sheets etc. all finished. I am now in a state of suspended animation waiting for the next thing to happen.

Saturday 10 April (Wedding Day) to Monday 26 April (Easter Monday) This is being written after I have been back at work for a week – and am beginning to be a little more reconciled to the idea. Terry arrived on the evening of the 9th, looking very nice in his maroon beret and very fit. [He had just been commissioned as a Second Lieutenant in the 2nd Battalion the Oxfordshire and Buckinghamshire Light Infantry, which was part of the 6th Airborne Division (in gliders). This Battalion had been the old 52nd Regiment, which fought its way through Spain under Wellington in the Peninsular War and at Waterloo; and whenever possible the historic old name was used.]

Saturday 10th was a hectic day, the climax of a hectic week. On Thursday we went out gathering green leaves from the hedges, and on Friday afternoon Shirley Deacon and I collected the flowers I had ordered to decorate the church and the house. As it was Lent, I could only put flowers in the vases on the altar, and even that was a favour. They had to be removed afterwards [and I arranged for them to be given] to a hospital. I arranged the presents in the breakfast-room on one half of the ping-pong table, suitably disguised. They made quite a good show. In the evening Terry had supper with us, and then he and I went to see the Vicar to run through the service. I'm afraid we rather disgraced ourselves by our giggling and general frivolity, but he didn't seem to mind. Terry took notes of everything and reduced it to a military operation – starting at zero hour and so on. I gave Terry the fountain pen I had managed to get for him, and he gave me some more Handel records. (I had had to get some of them myself because he couldn't find many in Morecambe.)

On Saturday morning I decorated Letitia's Cupid (from her wedding-cake) with forget-me-nots, and tied blue ribbon round the cake, on the door handles and everywhere else, including the cats, that I could think of. After that I had to dress in my new 'doe' [doeskin cloth, being the best official quality]. The service went without a hitch, and we both enjoyed it. I wasn't nervous, though I had rather expected to be. The organist played the wrong Allegro from the *Water Music* for me to go in, but he managed to get the *Trumpet Voluntary* all right for coming out. When we got to the porch, Fleur [Terry's small niece] was waiting with Jamie [a dog], also with

Terry and Audrey Deacon on their wedding day, 10 April 1943.

a blue bow, and gave me a tiny sprig of white heather. I was rather shattered to find the choir lined up and also a WRNS guard of honour, including the Superintendent. We duly posed for the photographer (Press) outside the church.

The service was at 1130. We had a reception and then left for Watchet at 1330 to catch the 1400 train. The cake, though it, of course, had to have chocolate icing instead of white [on account of rationing], was quite good, and looked very decorative with its two tiers. I cut it with a dagger lent to Terry by [a parachutist officer from his OCTU].

Warick was in our train as far as Taunton, where we had to change into a branch line train, arriving at Watchet about 1800. The West Somerset Hotel was very comfortable – not big or crowded, but very well run and with good cooking. We tried to look as if we'd been married for ages but I don't think it can have succeeded very well, especially when we kept receiving Press cuttings and photographs and photographers' proofs. Not to mention the greeting telegrams we had to add up and make a list of, for cake. We had a lovely holiday there. On Monday we walked to Dunster, via Blue Anchor and Carhampton; on Tuesday we went to Taunton for the afternoon and evening. Terry bought a raincoat, we saw half a film and then tried to get dinner. But the town was so full that we couldn't and were reduced to having a pasty at the station buffet! On Wednesday we did a fairly strenuous walk to the Quantocks behind St. Audries' Bay. It is very pretty country in all directions, with good views of the Bristol Channel and across to Wales. On Thursday we walked to St. Audries and sat on the beach there. It was so hot it seemed like midsummer. In the evening we had to pack – very reluctantly.

On Friday we travelled up to Little Missenden [This is a mistake for Amersham] for Terry to join his unit . . . I was to stay at the Badminton Court Hotel. In the evening, when I had unpacked, Terry was able to come and see me. Actually he arrived with permission to sleep out and the news that he had been sent to the wrong place, and would have to leave next morning for the right one – which he didn't yet know. The BC Hotel couldn't put him up, but said it would release my room if we could find other accommodation. So we walked up the road to the Crown and were able to book a room. We had dinner and then went back to BC for me to pack. Then back to the Crown – and unpack again!

Next morning we left with [another Second Lieutenant] from Terry's OCTU and also intended for his unit, for Bulford on Salisbury Plain. Between the three of us we had 13 pieces of luggage, which made crossing London something of an operation. We duly arrived at Bulford, and Terry and [his friend] went off to the camp, promising to ring up later. In the meantime, I had to find somewhere to stay. The local hotel had no catering permit, but they put me on to a cottage, where I was able to get a room. Once again Terry was given a sleeping-out pass and didn't have to go back till p.m. Sunday. It was really very funny – a tiny room and very primitive. There were two mirrors – to see in one you had to sit on the bed, and to see in the other you had to kneel on the floor. We were almost hysterical by the time we had finished. Had dinner at Amesbury at the George.

I came back to Plymouth very unwillingly on Monday morning, to go on duty for 14 hours at 1800, and again at 1800 next evening – due to the change of watches.

. . .Terry has given me his cap badge to have made into a brooch, which I'm hoping will be ready by my next week-end. On account of the change in watches, it comes round a week early, on 7 May.

Friday 7 May I went up to see Terry for the week-end, staying this time at Amesbury (Avon Hotel). I got there just before 2, travelling straight after night watch; and he arrived about half-past five, with a sleeping-out pass for Friday and Sunday and a 36 hours' pass from Saturday mid-day to Sunday midnight.

Saturday was cold and windy with heavy showers. In the morning I walked over to Bulford and got rather wet. Terry came for lunch and afterwards we tried to go to Salisbury, but missed the train and the buses were full, so we went to Andover instead. It is a hole, but we saw a 'flick' (*Moon and Sixpence*) and had a good dinner.

Sunday 9 May Cold and very windy but fine. In the morning we went to Amesbury Church, but didn't like the service – it was very High. In the afternoon we walked to Stonehenge, a distance of 3 miles. I was disappointed in it, having expected it to be much bigger. The photographs one sees are misleading. But it was very interesting. Quite a lot of people there, mostly Army.

Monday 10 May Terry had to leave by the 6.20 bus, which meant getting up at 5.30. A filthy morning with wind and heavy rain. I left by the 9.44, arriving Plymouth 1531. It was a lovely week-end. Terry rang up in the evening.

Thursday 13 May The fighting in North Africa is over, except for 'mopping up'.

Elsie invited me to the WRNS guest night; it was quite good fun in a mild way.

[see entry for 30 January 1943]

When the Train Goes

When the train goes
It takes with it the entire
Short life we have lived: we lose
The talking at dusk beside the fire,
Walking together in the winter wind,
Laughing, and silences when to stir
Only a finger was to speak and find
Answer enough in the mere
Sight of the other's dimlit brow.
All these it takes: they are
Swift gone as its steam. There is snow
In the wind, there are bare
Lines and bombed houses. The rest we lose,
We lose when the train goes.

CHAPTER II

WRNS in Quarters

Wednesday 26 May Terry is now doing a battle course in Derbyshire. I hope to be able to get there for my week-end.

Official dinner party at Penlee Gardens WRNS Quarters for the Director WRNS. I sat at her table but did not talk to her. Very good dinner but afterwards it was simply awful. Somebody played the piano and we vaguely sang. One frightful woman gave an allegedly comic recitation – *Sing a Song of Sixpence* in three different ways. Quite incredible. At 2300 I had a duty car call for me and went on duty . . . [In many ways people were astonishingly naive at that time; women in particular often led very sheltered lives, and many of those who joined the WRNS had never been away from home or held a job before. Wren Tapp (Mrs. Sears) describes life in ratings' quarters:-

'Discipline was far tighter than most girls of today would be ready to accept. Twenty-one was the age of majority, and the officers of the armed services are traditionally regarded as being *in loco parentis* in respect of all members who are minors. This discipline was applied to all other ranks in the WRNS without regard to age or marital status. We were locked up in our quarters at ten every evening. To be a few seconds adrift was as much of a crime as to be overdue for some hours. Indeed, I can still recall the indignation I felt on being "bottled" [lectured] by a Wren Petty Officer for "cutting things a bit fine" when I walked through the door as the Town Hall commenced to strike the hour. Two late passes to eleven o'clock were allowed per week. These had to be pre-arranged and not taken for granted. We were obliged to report to the Regulating Office on our going out and on our coming in.

'Cheating, though not unknown, was not generally practised. For a start, blackout arrangements added to the hazard of climbing through windows. [To black-out the windows portable shields made of hardboard, or thick curtains, were affixed to the inside to prevent lights showing.] I was once asked for my co-operation in the matter of climbing my cabin window when some of the others realized it was at the head of the fire escape. Not only that, but the Leading Wren with whom I shared it was watchkeeping, and usually only turned in as we were leaving for duty. The answer to this problem was simple. I invited the would-be miscreants to listen to the booted footsteps of the sentry as he passed to and fro on the gravel path below. As St. Mary's was not exactly Colditz, it was agreed the risk was hardly worth the taking. If we went out to a cinema or other place of public entertainment, to a canteen or any other service mess, and most particularly to an American base, we had to wear uniform. This applied whether we were unaccompanied or in a group with other Wrens or servicemen.

'A special extension to twelve o'clock was allowed for any event organized by the Americans if our attendance had Regulating Office approval. As we all had to get back by the transport provided, there being absolutely no other, there was little or no chance of our going adrift and reporting back late.

'Despite this rigid regulation of our liberty, which was of course unremarkable in time of war, the WRNS was not in fact subject to Naval law and discipline. This meant that, for instance, we had the privilege of wearing civilian clothes when off duty except in the cases already mentioned. The humane attitude behind this dispensation arose from the fact that so many girls in the service had been recruited from Naval families, and it set aside the disciplinary difficulties that would otherwise have arisen if Wren ratings in uniform were seen out with husbands, brothers, fathers or boy friends in officers' uniform.

'. . .In our leisure time handicrafts were actively encouraged. A special issue of craft materials was made available from time to time. Embroidery kits and tapestries were especially welcome, and we would sit around in the evenings, usually in our dressing gowns, sewing and knitting and nattering. It all sounds cosier than it was, but most of us had grown up in austere circumstances even without the War.

'With the arrival of the D-day summer [1944] all leave was cancelled, and particular emphasis given to organizing our leisure. There were competitions and displays of our work. I was delighted to have an award for a becoming green dress I had made. It was hand sown, every stitch, as there was no sewing machine in our quarters. Undeniably, though, the first prize in that competition was earned by our First Officer for her patchwork quilt. She was a Canadian and we all loved her. She had a strong physical resemblance to Queen Elizabeth the Queen Mother, and we felt that in our Queen Bee we had the next best thing to the present Queen Mum.'

There were of course some embarrassing pregnancies; but the only one of which I had direct personal knowledge concerned a Third Officer who was well into her thirties. She was quietly discharged, as usual with all pregnancies, married or otherwise, but there was no prospect of marriage, and the whole episode seemed singularly joyless in all respects.

There were one or two stories – probably invented, or at least embroidered – such as that of the steward who waited on her Surgeon Commander at dinner one evening, and then gave birth the following day, to his alleged complete astonishment. Years of experience of dealing with sailors had not prepared him for that sort of thing. A good many tales were told too, involving the exploits of amorous Americans, and the amusing one about a Norwegian sailor who paid several visits stark naked to the WRNS quarters near his own naval accommodation at Plymouth.

CHAPTER III

Interludes

Friday 4 June After night-watch I went up to Derbyshire. A fighter plane hit the train just before we got to Taunton and crashed in flames in a field near the line. There was nothing to be seen of it or the pilot – just a cloud of smoke and flame. When we arrived at Taunton we found that a Wren had been hurt. She was naturally turned over to us [I was travelling with Third Officer Barbara Morgan] and we did what we could for her till an ambulance came. She was not seriously injured, but rather badly shaken. Barbara stayed with her to see her into hospital and send wires for her, and I went on in the hope of getting my connection at Bristol.

After changing trains again at Bridgwater, I arrived at Bristol ten minutes late – just in time to see the other train go out. There were two women in my carriage also going north, so after we had sent wires to our destinations, we went out to get lunch in the town. We were directed to the Grosvenor Hotel, but found that its restaurant was closed. However, we were told that we could get sandwiches in the bar, so we went in there and tried to order them. There was a Scotsman at the bar drinking whisky (slightly tight) who announced that he was the manager and refused to let us pay. It turned out that he wasn't the manager but a merchant seaman on leave! The train I finally got, two hours after the right one, got gradually later as it went. It had started to rain and the further we went, the wetter it seemed to be – most depressing – I had visions of missing the last bus from Chesterfield etc., etc. [The train] arrived late at 2020; but luckily Terry's night scheme had been cancelled and he met me at Chesterfield Station and we managed to get a bus to Heath, followed by a walk across the fields to Stainsby. By then I'd had just about all I wanted for one day.

I stayed at a small farm, with a family of very North Country and very kind people. Terry stayed there too each night. In fact the only time he was away was Saturday morning, when he had to do the assault course. But that was over by 1130, so he had lunch with me and then we went into Chesterfield. We did a 'flick', *Somewhere I'll Find You*, and then had a very good dinner (lobster salad or salmon) at the Station Hotel.

On Sunday morning it poured with rain, but in the afternoon it cleared and we went for a walk through the grounds of Hardwick Hall, taking

Teddy the cow-dog with us. It is pretty country and lovely trees. However there were coal mines all round in every direction, though not in the immediate neighbourhood of Stainsby. On Sunday evening we went for another walk, after seeing the foal – very young – who came up and licked my hand. He was very pretty. I had to leave by the 0800 bus from Heath on Monday, which meant getting up at 0600. Terry carried my case for me and then went back to the camp for breakfast. I had a very comfortable journey back, arriving just before 1900.

Tuesday 8 June Winston Churchill is back from the US and has spoken in the House of Commons about his visit to Washington, followed by Gibraltar and Algiers. The [WRNS] cypherers who went from here come back to-morrow.

Friday 12 June Terry arrived at 0600, having managed to get a 36-hour pass on his way from Derbyshire to Ilfracombe. He left by the 1650 train on Saturday. I hope to see him while he is so near. . .

Thursday 24 June I went by the 0830 bus to Barnstaple to see Terry, who had a free day. It was a wonderfully fine day and really hot. After lunch we basked in the sun by the river in our shirt sleeves. I had to leave again by the 1742 bus (the last?) from Bideford, so Terry went back with me as far as Bideford Quay. In spite of going straight after night watch (one hour's sleep), I didn't feel very tired.

Friday 25 June The RAF has been bombing the Ruhr very heavily; the Germans no longer attempt to make light of the raids. It is a ghastly business.

Thursday 1 July Having done a swap with Alison[1], I went off by the 1650 train to Ilfracombe, where I was able to stay until the last train (1645!) on Friday. Terry had a sleeping-out pass and had booked bed and breakfast at a comic boarding-house – the only place available. The woman was stone deaf. I never managed to make her hear a word. In the morning I went down to the sea front to watch Terry drill his platoon. After that I bought some food to take on our picnic – sausage rolls, a lettuce and some radishes, tuffs [alias tough cakes, a local form of bread roll] and fish paste and buns. Terry was free from just after half past ten, and we walked to the

1. Third (later Second) Officer A.M. Rowatt.

cove beyond Rapparee. We lay in the sun and bathed, and lay in the sun again till 3 o'clock, when we had to leave. It was a beautiful day and I hated going back, particularly as I had a night watch before me.

Saturday 3 July I stayed at home this week-end, because Terry was [able to come here] on his way back to Bulford. Today we took the morning train to King Tor and walked to Great Mistor. In the course of my looking round, I saw hut circles above the River Walkham and went down to see them. There were two groups, the one I looked at consisting of a series of joined circles enclosing groups of beehive huts. The perimeter, built of loose stone-walling, was about two feet high, and the best-preserved hut walls were about three feet high. On the way back we crossed another hut circle site and two parallel double stone rows about thirty yards apart, each consisting of two parallel rows of upright stones and running east and west. It was again a marvellously hot day and we came home the colour of Red Indians.

Thursday 8 July ...A party of us went to the Palace Theatre to see Noel Coward in his *Present Laughter*. It is very clever and well acted, but not my type at all: too artificial ... On Monday he and Judy Campbell had given a performance at the Royal Marine Barracks [which had its own small theatre] of songs and recitations, and been entertained to tea.

Monday 12 July ...Our leave started today. I met Terry at Okehampton and we were able to get a room in a rather nice guest house – full of maiden ladies of both sexes. We were very comfortable and the food was good.

Tuesday 13 July We walked via Belstone to Cawsand Beacon, where we ate our sandwiches, and then to South Zeal and back along the road through Sticklepath. About eleven miles and quite a good walk. It threatened to rain but didn't, apart from one shower, and on the way back the sun was hot. In the evening we saw the most hopeless film we've even seen – a revival of *Caravan*. We walked out halfway through.

Wednesday 14 July We walked to Branscombe's Loaf (on Sourton Common), skirting Yes Tor and High Willhays and crossing the West Okement. The latter was rather fun: the only way I could get across the last bit was by getting on Terry's back and using him as a bridge [he had learned this technique during his assault training.] It was a windy day with intermittent drizzle and on the way back rain set in steadily. About 12–13 miles, and really rather strenuous – there was so much up and down.

Thursday 15 July Wet morning, but cleared temporarily after lunch. We set out to walk along the Hatherleigh road, but got so soaking wet that we had to turn back before we reached anywhere in particular. We had an enormous tea on the way back and didn't seem to be any the worse. In the evening we saw the film *Squadron Leader X*.

Friday 16 July In the morning the sun was really hot, so we just lay on Okehampton Common and basked until it was time to go and pack. We then found that I had looked up the wrong train and had to get dinner in the town while we waited. All the hotels were full and we ended in a funny little cafe, where we had bacon, sausage and chips.

Monday 19 July Letitia's birthday. We went to the Anglo-Polish ballet – *Polonica, Umarl Maciek Umarl* and the inevitable *Krakow Wedding*. Nothing much over the week-end – vague walks. On Saturday miniature billiards and supper . . . next door, also a hearty thunderstorm; Sunday church and vague walks.

Wednesday 21 July Terry's leave ended, but I travelled back with him to Amesbury, having till Monday left. He was able to get away each evening before dinner and to sleep out, having to catch the 6.20 bus each morning. On Saturday we went to Salisbury directly after lunch, did some shopping, had tea, went to a 'flick' and had an excellent dinner at the Red Lion. On Sunday he was free all day. In the morning we walked over Bulford for mattins, and did nothing much during the remainder of the day. Both of us feeling the end of our leave. It was the longest time we have had together.

Monday 26 July Mussolini has resigned.
    I said good-bye to Terry at 0615 and came home (very reluctantly) by my usual train, which was very hot and crowded. Duty at midnight.

Wednesday 28 July I had to wash a lot of clothes this morning – the usual aftermath of leave – which was very tiring, because it was such a stuffy day. Then I went to have the test for ultra-violet-ray treatment, which is to be given to those of us who work underground. It consisted of a three-minute skin test and of being weighed. Weight (without shoes and jacket) exactly 10 stone – 2lb less than when I was pulmographed last year.

[We had by now been working for a considerable time in the underground headquarters, with artificial light and ventilation. This building was, in effect, at the bottom of the Commander in Chief's garden; so that if it was considered that the Admiral ought to see a particular signal late in the evening, one of us had to take it up to the house, through the dark grounds, to the drawing-room full of light and flowers – feeling rather like a Nibelung emerging from his cave. Signals of certain special types had to be shown immediately to an appropriate naval officer – sometimes the Commander on duty in the Operations Room, sometimes the Duty Captain, who had a cabin attached to his office and could turn in for an hour or two when things were quiet at night. This could lead to odd incidents, such as the occasion when I went down with one of these special messages and found him in his shirt, with his trousers over his arm. No eyelid was batted by either party, and we conducted a perfectly normal conversation.]

Thursday 29 July Very hot day, most enervating. I have rarely been as hot and tired as I was when I got home after this afternoon's watch. I am working with 'D' watch till Monday, having swapped week-ends with Alison.

Three minutes back and front ultra-violet treatment this morning.

Friday 30 July Even hotter, with a kind of damp stuffy feeling, even though it is bright and clear. Not the sort of weather for work.

I had to pay 4/6d for a perfectly normal comb, having broken my old one. Yesterday I paid 3/6d for a metal soap-box.

CHAPTER IV

WRNS at the Quebec, Cairo and Tehran Conferences

Wednesday 11 August Churchill has arrived in Canada [for the Quebec Conference]. Tonight, or rather early Thursday morning, we had an air raid much on the lines of the last [not mentioned] except that as far as we were concerned, there were more incendiaries than HE's. I put out three – two with sand, one with a dustbin lid. There were dozens in the road and gardens, and the houses each side of us had one through their roofs. One bungalow burned out. It was a clear moonlit night, as before. [In fact this was a serious raid, with 41 killed and 160 injured.[1]]

Saturday 14 August C. in C.'s[2] farewell cocktail party. Masses of gold lace present: not bad as these things go. Saw some people I hadn't seen since I was a rating.

Feel as if I'm starting 'flu or something, aching all over, sore throat, headache and probable temperature.

Sunday 15 August Rome has been declared an open city, after two (I think) bombing attacks. The raids on Hamburg seem to have been terribly effective. The city has apparently ceased to exist for practical purposes. It is a grisly business.

Still feeling rather ill. Siren tonight but nothing happened. Again a lovely night.

Friday 20 August . . .I had a postcard from Pat and Joy in Quebec, where they are attached to the delegation. [They had been selected to form part of the cypher staff for the conference.] It was written on the 15th, so it must have come over by air in some special way – ordinary air mail takes a few weeks.

Sunday 22 August Terry rang up this evening to say that he has a scheme

---

1. Twyford.
2. Admiral of the Fleet Sir Charles Forbes.

next week-end – which is the one when I would have been able to go and see him. It is very disappointing.

Thursday 26 August I have tried to swap week-ends, but without success. Terry rang up again to ask if I had had any luck.

Friday 27 August I had more or less resigned myself to a wasted week-end and had gone to bed as usual after night watch, when at 1230 Terry rang up to say that he thought the scheme was cancelled. I decided to take a chance and caught the 2.30 train. I was very glad I did so, because it turned out that the scheme (at Bournemouth) was cancelled, which meant that we could have a normal week-end together. Stayed at the Avon Hotel [Amesbury] this time. Terry had had a hectic week, with 60 miles marching since Monday; his feet were covered in blisters. He gave me a lovely book: the Phaidon Press *Rembrandt.*

The Quebec Conferences are finished. Roosevelt has gone back to the States and Churchill is having a short holiday in Canada. Lord Louis Mountbatten[1], Chief of Combined Operations, has been appointed to the command of Allied forces in South-east Asia. It is a supreme command, like that of Eisenhower.

Tuesday 31 August Marjorie Warden's[2] farewell party. She is going to *Excellent* as a Chief Officer.

Thursday 2 September Went to guest night at Thornhill Road at Elsie's invitation. [This consisted of several small houses taken over for use as WRNS officers' quarters. At one stage, with the constant increase in numbers, they became overfull, being particularly short of common-room space. This was important, because bedrooms had to be shared. The difficulty was overcome by inviting the Signal Officer to dinner one evening, making sure that every one off duty – from all departments – was in. The point was taken; presumably representations were made in appropriate places, and additional accommodation was provided.]

Friday 3 September . . .Four years ago today Great Britain declared war on Germany, who had attacked Poland on 1 September. The day was observed as a National Day of Prayer.

---

1. Lord Louis (1900–1979); later 1st Earl Mountbatten of Burma; last Viceroy of India 1947; assassinated 1979.
2. First Officer, in charge of WRNS personnel in ACHQ. H.M.S. *Excellent* meant Portsmouth.

Looking back to 1939, one feels that we were different people then. Neville Chamberlain was Prime Minister, General Gamelin[1] was C. in C. Allied Armies, and the Maginot Line was considered impregnable. There was a ridiculous song: 'We're going to hang out the washing on the Siegfried Line' [The German equivalent of the Maginot Line]. One thought that every soldier would immediately go to France. Terry went as far as Dorset, after we had said pathetic farewells, and used for a time to get home quite often. It all seems very far away now. I went out to lunch with Priscilla. In the afternoon saw a stupid film, *Cargo of Innocents*, and a rather good documentary about Greece, *Greek Testament*.

Wednesday 8 September Italy has surrendered unconditionally. . .

Saturday 11 September I cannot help feeling sorry for the Italians; it seems that they are going to have a very hard time. The Germans have occupied most of the North, not without resistance by the Italian army, and after having bombarded Rome, have occupied key points in the city, including the radio transmitter, and have 'taken over the protection of Vatican City'. British and American troops have landed in force south of Naples and are in contact with the Germans, and British naval forces have occupied Taranto . . . Battleships, cruisers and destroyers of the Italian fleet have reached Malta, in response to Admiral Cunningham's[2] appeal to them to escape . . . Hitler has broadcast a speech declaring that Badoglio and the King of Italy have betrayed Germany, and also saying that Italy's capitulation makes no military difference because Germany has been doing most of the fighting anyway.

Churchill is still in Washington. Arrangements are being made for a meeting with Stalin. . .

Spent the day in bed with a heavy cold, feeling rather guilty.

Friday 24 September . . .Churchill is back in this country and has spoken in Parliament on the progress of the War.

. . .The Foreign Secretary has told the story behind the arrival of Hess in this country some two years ago. [10 May 1941]. It appears that he came with peace proposals, including 'a free hand' for Germany in Europe and the return of the former German colonies, while Russia should be regarded as part of Asia. In return we were to be allowed to keep the

---

1. Maurice Gustave Gamelin (1872–1958).
2. Andrew Brown Cunningham (1883–1963); later 1st Viscount Cunningham of Hyndhope. Admiral of the Fleet; Commander in Chief, Allied Forces in Mediterranean.

British Empire. The alternative, if we refused, was that the Führer would consider it his duty to exterminate us.

Very good party at Penny's[1] last Sunday, followed by a meal at a funny little place called the AEL.

This morning went up to Amesbury for the week-end. Our watches are due to change again next week, so I get another week-end in a fortnight's time. Very pleasant week-end, as usual. Went into Salisbury on Saturday afternoon.

Tuesday 28 September I found on my going on duty that Penny was in hospital as the result of a bicycle crash on Friday morning. This morning I did not go to bed, but after having a bath and sun-ray [both at ACHQ] went shopping (grapes and flowers). In the afternoon I went to see Penny, who was very cheerful in spite of a cracked bone in her right shoulder and a very badly bruised face. She will be in RNH [hospital] till the end of the week and will then go on leave. I do not know when she will be able to go back to duty.

Friday 8 October Pat and Joy came back [from the Quebec Conference] this week, with presents for everybody from Canada and US – all beautifully packed and looking quite pre-war. They had a wonderful time, though they had to work hard. Most of the time they were in Quebec, and then in Washington for a little while. They came back in the *Renown* with Churchill.

I went up to Amesbury again today for the week-end.

Somewhat to our dismay, the personnel of the watches is being shuffled round. Fortunately I keep Joy and Penny, but Pat and Brita have had to go into other watches.

...On Saturday we went to Salisbury, this time with a friend of Terry's, Gordon Groos. Most of the time we spent in an interminable argument about the moon and the tides. All rather good fun. It was a lovely warm day, and a bright moonlit evening when we came back.

On Sunday morning we walked over to Bulford for church. By lunchtime the sun had come out and it was really quite hot. We spent the afternoon sitting by the river on a tree stump. The air was still, and the water smooth as glass, reflecting the trees and the people crossing by the bridge. Two swans stayed almost motionless in mid-stream all the time we were there and the waterfowl bustled in and out of the reeds, squawking

---

1. Third (later Second) Officer, Mrs. C.B. Alers-Hankey.

occasionally. The leaves were turning yellow and beginning to fall. There are many willows by the Avon here, and aspens and poplars. The leaves of the willows fell one by one, twirling slowly down. It was so peaceful that one felt almost stupid with calmness and content. In the evening we were lent bicycles and rode through woods and over part of the Plain in the cool air. By the time we came back the mist was rising and the sun was setting a wintry red. Terry's leave starts in a fortnight's time.

Tuesday 9 November Having just had nine days' leave, followed by a week-end with Terry, I am very much behind with all this.

We spent our leave here [Plymouth] going out for days. One day we walked round Burrator Lake, through Meavy and back to Yelverton; another walk took us from Roborough through Tamerton Foliot home. We also bicycled out to Yealmpton and one day Terry went for a 10-mile run. I went with him on a bicycle ... He gave me some lovely records for my birthday – Brandenburg Concerto no. 5, played by Thibaud, Cortot and Cortet, and Mozart concerto in D, played by Menuhin and the Liverpool Philharmonic Orchestra.

On the 4th I went back for two watches and then went up to see him for the week-end. He was on duty on Friday night on an exercise, and I didn't get to Bulford till 2230 (having looked up the wrong train), so I didn't see him till the morning. It was a frightful place he'd booked at, and when he got there and saw it in daylight he said we couldn't stay there. So we went to Salisbury and tried to find somewhere there. Every hotel was full in Salisbury and Harnham, but after spending the entire afternoon trailing round, we found quite a nice place for bed and breakfast. In the evening we had dinner at the Red Lion with the Padre and [another friend from Terry's unit] Clifford (who had recommended the filthy place at Bulford) and his girl-friend. By that time Terry was feeling pretty tired. I was myself and I had had a night's rest. I've never seen him so tired. In the morning he got up late and I brought our breakfast up on a tray. We went to the Red Lion for lunch, which wasn't exactly a success, because by the time we got to the meat course the beefsteak pie was off, and there was calf's head, jugged hare and stewed rabbit [none of which either of us could bear]. So we just had soup, sweet and bread and cheese. In the afternoon we walked out to Wilton, ate a huge tea and walked back again. It was fine but very cold. In the morning we were miserably cold walking round the Close and so on in Salisbury. We had a slap-up dinner (roast pheasant) at the White Hart – so at least we ended well!

Terry had to get the 7 o'clock bus on the Monday morning. I came back as usual by the 1107, which was so full I had to sit on my case till I got to Bere Alston.

Friday 12 November This afternoon, coming off at 1300, I had to take a 'hand of officer' signal to two ships in the Sound. I went in Captain Gandell's[1] barge, manned by three Wrens. [This was, of course, a small but fairly fast motor-boat. The job of boat's crew was one of the most coveted among WRNS ratings. Wearing bell-bottomed trousers, the girls looked very smart and took great pride in handling their boats, wielding their boathooks with skill in order to come nearly alongside jetty or ship. These particular girls apologized to me for the slightly rough sea!]

It was quite a thrill, especially going aboard and the saluting as we arrived and left. One big ship and one not quite so big. Met Joy and Pat on the former (*Renown*). [The name of the ship was added later. This entry, worded guardedly as it had to be at the time, indicates, taken with the entries for 28 November and 27 December, that Pat and Joy were among the WRNS forming part of the staff accompanying Churchill to the Cairo Conference. Some members of the WRNS group also went to Tehran for the second Conference.]

Tuesday 16 November Short raid this morning at 0500. Our house was undamaged, but bombs were dropped near – one just by one of the Wrens' quarters. [Casualties in the town were 18 killed and about 60 injured[2].

Wednesday 17 November . . .It has been very cold during the past two or three days; there was snow on the moor. Today I slept (after night duty) till 1815 – the longest I have ever done – I suppose on account of our early call yesterday. We didn't go back to bed after the raid, but had breakfast about 0600. I had to go on duty at 0800.

Sunday 28 November . . .Considerable feeling has been caused by the release of Sir Oswald Mosley[3], formerly leader of the British Union of Fascists, who was detained under the famous Regulation 18B in 1940 (?). (The release was on the grounds of his ill-health, and is subject to fairly comprehensive restrictions). Various Trade Unions have protested to the Home Secretary; and a statement has been made in Parliament explaining the position. While I have not made up my mind, and in any case I'm very

1. Captain W.P. Gandell, CBE.
2. Twyford.
3. Sir Oswald Ernald Mosley (1896–1980); founded British Union of Fascists in 1930's.

On the quarterdeck of HMS Renown, September, 1943: WRNS cypher officers who accompanied Winston Churchill and his party during his visit to Canada and the United States (including a meeting with President Roosevelt). Left to right: Second Officer Doris Richardson, Second Officer Dorina Wood, Third Officer Pat Ommanney, Third Officer Joy Hope, Third Officer Judy Love, Third Officer Elizabeth Gibson, First Officer Jean Davies, Third Officer Ann Relf, Third Officer Dorothy Davis and Third Officer Doreen Drax. [By courtesy of the Trustees, Imperial War Museum.]

far from being pro-Mosley, I think that surely this is one of the things we're alleged to be fighting for – the reasonably just handling of the case even of people one doesn't agree with.

The papers keep saying that a meeting between Churchill, Roosevelt and Stalin is expected any minute now; but nothing has been announced.

In the office we have been suffering from an epidemic of 'flu'. For about a fortnight all the watches have been short-handed (in addition to other reasons) and life has been pretty strenuous.

Friday 3 December My week-end again. Thank Heaven I didn't get 'flu and have to stay at home. However, I started a cold on my way up and felt pretty wretched during the evening. This time we stayed at the Manor Private Hotel, Durrington – rather nice. It was, as usual, horribly cold.

Saturday 4 December As usual I met Terry after lunch and we went into Salisbury for the afternoon and evening. For once we saw a good film, *Watch on the Rhine*. I was thoroughly spoiled by being given my breakfast in bed, including an egg, without asking for it. I didn't get up till nearly eleven, and felt much better for it.

Sunday 5 December When I woke up this morning, I found my cold had gone, much to my joy. We went to church in the morning, and in the afternoon went for a rather pleasant walk through Milston, Brigmerston and Figheldean, accompanied by the hotel dog. We were thoroughly childish and trod on all the puddles to hear the ice crack. In the evening we did Christmas cards.

The time went very quickly and I hated coming back.

Tuesday 7 December Churchill and Roosevelt have had a Conference with Chiang Kai Shek[1] in Egypt, and then went on to Tehran for a four-day talk with Stalin. A joint declaration has been issued. During their meetings Churchill presented Stalin with the Sword of Honour given by the King to Stalingrad. It had previously been shown in many places (including Plymouth, but I missed seeing it).

Saturday 18 December . . .Churchill, who is ill with pneumonia somewhere in the Middle East, is said to be getting better. Mrs. Churchill has flown out to him.

---

1. Chiang Kai Shek (1887–1975); President of China 1928–50. The Communist victory limited his rule to Formosa (Taiwan).

The 'flu epidemic is said to have passed its peak; it certainly has so far as the cypher office is concerned. There have been epidemics not only in this country but also in Germany and America. This afternoon I went to the City Hospital to see Elsie, who had had her appendix taken out on Tuesday. She was looking better than she did before the operation.

This week I managed to get a copy of *War and Peace*, which I ordered last February. Even now I should not have had it if someone else had not decided she did not want her copy.

Monday 27 December Having gone into three watches over Christmas – so as to let 'B' [watch] have their week-end two days earlier, on account of the travelling ban for the Services – I have hardly come to the surface till today. On Christmas Eve we worked morning and evening – the latter being the worst watch I've ever known. We were frantically busy, and on top of that everything went wrong. I finally disgraced myself by bursting into tears. It was awful. On Christmas Day we worked afternoon and night. I had to see Staff Officer (Signals)[1] about the cyphering mistakes yesterday [as head of the watch I had of course to accept responsibility] – he was really quite pleasant about it. . .

I had quite a few presents – a tray, records (a suite by John Field) and the music of Peer Gynt from 'the Mayor' and Letitia, savings stamps from Warick, guide to Dartmoor from Lois[2], soap from Shirley, *Landworkers* [a poem] from Berenice and a painted jar from Mrs. Deacon. Terry sent me a tiny bottle of scent – I can't think where he got it – and is going to give me another cap badge to replace the original one, which I lost during our last leave.

On Boxing Day I slept till tea-time, when [the people from next door came in]. Roger and [his mother] slept here, because [his father] had to go on duty with his Home Guard anti-aircraft unit. Rather a pleasant evening playing gramophone records. I had intended to go to church on either Christmas Day or Sunday, but somehow there wasn't time and I was tired and lazy.

General Eisenhower, US Army, has been appointed C. in C. of the forces organizing in this country, with General Montgomery (8th Army) in command of the British forces. General Alexander[3] is to command in Italy, and General Maitland Wilson[4] in the Mediterranean as a whole.

1. Commander (later Captain) F.B. Tours OBE.
2. Terry's eldest sister.
3. Harold Rupert Leofric George Alexander (1891–1969); later Field-Marshal; 1st Earl Alexander of Tunis; Supreme Allied Commander Mediterranean.
4. Henry Maitland Wilson (1881–1964); later Field-Marshal; 1st Baron Maitland Wilson.

Churchill is getting better. There are no regular bulletins. . .

We had a chicken for Christmas – by means of ordering it last year from Lois Hoskin.

Pat and Joy are back from Cairo and Tehran [Conferences] – Joy did not go to the latter. Working very hard.

Tuesday 28 December . . .I have never known anything like the pressure of work during the past two days. [Press cuttings describe an air–sea action in the Bay of Biscay, in which HM Ships *Glasgow* and *Enterprise* with aircraft of Coastal Command and the US Navy, sank three German destroyers and damaged others. This obviously resulted in a greatly increased number of operational messages being handled. . .]

Friday 31 December My week-end. I had to travel up to Salisbury with the Director's young sons, at Mrs. Welby's request. [Terry and I] stayed this time at Durrington, in a little house in the village. In the evening we went to a New Year's dance given by the sergeants of the 52nd and (for the first time in my life!) saw the New Year in. Met a lot of Terry's friends. We walked there and back, and having had no rest the previous night, I was just about ready for bed by the time we got back, just after one, though I had slept a little after tea. . .

1944

CHAPTER I

Preparing for the Second Front

Durrington

Saturday 1 January I did not bother about breakfast, but slept on till just before lunch-time. As usual, I met Terry at Bulford Station and we went into Salisbury for the afternoon and evening. For the first time since the War I saw some crumpets and had to buy some for tea to-morrow. Also tried to buy a toothbrush, but without success. They are hard to get now. We saw the film, *The Lamp Still Burns*, but did not think it particularly good. On our way back we collected Terry's rations from the mess – an incredibly large amount. [Since this time we were staying in a private house and not a catering establishment, it was possible – indeed necessary – for him to take the food he would have been entitled to eat if resident in the mess. Service rations were more generous than civilian ones.]

Sunday 2 January Went to Durrington Church this morning. In the afternoon we went for a walk, and came back and toasted our crumpets by the fire. We had a sitting-room to ourselves.

Tuesday 4 January As usual I came back feeling as if I had been in another world, and having completely lost touch with the war news. . .

Sunday 9 January . . .Russia has published proposals for the settlement of the frontiers [of Poland]. They are based on the 'Curzon Line', which approximately corresponds to the limit of Russian occupation after the defeat of Poland by Germany, plus a large salient north of Warsaw . . . It is proposed to compensate Poland for loss of territory on the east by giving her German territory on the west.

   I do not see why Russia should claim so much in the east; though of course Poland has at times been aggressive towards her and is not politically wise. The proposal to give Poland German territory seems to be insane, and to contain the seeds of the next war. Unfortunately we seem to favour the Russian plan. We are, of course, not in a position to tell Russia where she gets off – she has a very forceful answer. I cannot remember whether under our guarantee to Poland in 1939 we promised to maintain her then frontiers.

A good deal of interest has been aroused by the announcement of a projected jet-propulsion aeroplane. It has no propeller, but proceeds by drawing in air at the nose, heating and compressing it, and allowing it to escape at the tail. Successful test flights have been made, and with its good powers of climbing and operating at great heights, the new plane is said to promise very well. It is a pleasantly quaint idea, anyway – invented by a RAF officer, Group Captain Whittle.

Tuesday 18 January Churchill is back in London.

Thursday 20 January This being Merchant Navy Week, we went to a free Service showing of the film *San Demetrio, London*. It is based on the story of the tanker of that name, sailing in the convoy attacked by a surface raider in which the Armed Merchant Cruiser *Jervis Bay* went down – which was hit by shellfire, abandoned on fire and later re-boarded and brought back to this country under her own power. It was a good film, simply told, without the usual propaganda nonsense and also the standard commercial love-interest.

[There is no further entry until 1 May. A note added later reads: 'Nothing of interest except a lot of hard work during this interval.' It was, of course, a period of tremendous pressure: in addition to the 'ordinary' operational work, which itself intensified, there were almost daily landing exercises for British and US forces at Slapton in South Devon; and since everything connected with the plans for the invasion of Normandy was secret, all the signals to ships and establishments involved had to pass through the cypher office.

I was promoted to Acting First Officer and placed in charge of the cypher office. This meant that I worked daily from 0900 to 1900 or later, and was responsible for seeing that all secret signals in and out were dealt with properly, in accordance with the Duty Officer's instructions, and copies distributed to everyone who needed them, plus general organization and oversight of the work of the 47 officers and 24 rating typists. One of these, whom I remember with affection, was Leading Wren Sylvia Grashoff, attached to 'A' watch. A plump girl with a mass of fair hair, her face invariable smudged from the purple carbon paper used for typing the master copies of signals, she was most efficient and could always be relied on to query anything she had to type which did not make sense. Off duty, she had a string of American boy-friends, whom she kept severely in order.

'Men have for so long cherished a belief that women can never keep a secret, yet many thousands of "Wrens" were engaged in the work of Preparation for "Neptune" [the sea-borne part of the invasion] and they proved themselves at least as "secure" as naval officers of considerable experience and training. The naval commander of one of the assault forces wrote in his report: "Nor must the work of the WRNS officers and ratings be forgotten. In spite of working very long hours, they remained keen and cheerful, and I knew of no instance of even the smallest lapse of security in spite of the fact that the majority of them had access to all Top Secret papers from the beginning. It must be remembered that most of the cypher staffs dealing with 'most secret' signals, and as well as the typists, teleprinter operators and others were "Wrens".'[1]

It was often difficult to remember what information one had seen in secret reports and what in the newspaper. People must often have thought us dim-witted for seeming to know so little about current events. There was one occasion when I went to lunch with friends and had to sit dumb while they discussed what to me were unmentionably secret arrangements for equipping a certain hutted camp for use by the US Navy. The reason for this having become common knowledge was that the Post Office staff concerned with installing the necessary telephones regarded it as a routine job and were under no obligation to treat it as secret. On the actual plans for the invasion – 'First Officer Margaret Drummond[2] (later to be Director WRNS) was Head of Section in the office of the Commander in Chief, Plymouth, dealing with the paper work for the invasion. Two months before D-day she received 20 copies of the Naval Plan and almost slept with them. She and her WRNS staff were responsible for issuing charts, typing and issuing sailing orders [all beginning with the resounding words "Being in all respects ready for sea and prepared to engage the enemy. . ."] and the allocation of berths to ships. They knew all that was going on[3].'

Throughout the two years during which the preliminary work was in progress, her deputy was Priscilla Chase, who was made MBE for her work. In conversations with the present writer she has described the increasing pressure of work over that period, reaching its climax early in 1944, and its absorbing interest – including, of course, meeting many

1. Edwards.
2. Dame Margaret Drummond, DBE.
3. Stuart Mason.

members of British and US forces who were to take part in the invasion. On a lighter note, she recalls her mystification, long before D-day, on seeing among the operational papers a document headed 'Secret – Self-heating soap' – seemingly a most improbable secret weapon. With the approach of the invasion, of course, the reason for the secrecy became clear.

During the early months of 1944 the preparations gathered momentum. The War Correspondent of *The Western Morning News* writes: 'Along our coasts, particularly up in the Slapton area of South Devon, where the coast, for a stretch of about seven miles and to an inland depth of about four miles, was completely evacuated of all civilians, for exclusive use by the United States' troops for sea-borne invasion practice of the most realistic kind, there were astonishing scenes. Great fleets of landing craft would charge in from the sea with men and equipment, and practise with grim resolution the part which they would soon be playing on the other side of the Channel . . . Huge convoys of landing craft . . . could be seen from the cliffs tossing and manoeuvring out in the Channel in varying weather.[1]']

---

1. Twyford.

CHAPTER II

A Tragic Accident

Monday 1 May Today I was sent for from Tidworth Military Families Hospital, where Terry has been taken after an accident. When I arrived I found that he had been hit in the neck by a splinter from a PIAT [anti-tank projectile] during a practice shoot. It struck the carotid artery and he lost a lot of blood. They gave him a transfusion, but his condition was still serious. When I arrived, late at night, he was asleep, but I was able to look at him. I slept that night at the hospital, and next day they found me accommodation in Tidworth. [With a retired colonel and his wife, who were doing this regularly, without charge, to help relatives of people taken to the hospital.]

Terry was quite conscious but very weak, and had some difficulty in finding his words – but he was wonderfully cheerful considering his condition. For the first few days he had only lemon and glucose, and he found difficulty in swallowing even that. But on Friday he suddenly started normal food and seemed much better, though even then, and till Monday 8th, when I had to return to Plymouth, his eyes could not focus well enough to read and his speech was not fluent. I hated leaving him, poor darling, in such a helpless state. He is very brave and very sweet.

The fragment of bomb they propose to leave in his neck, because they think it would do more harm than good to operate.

Tuesday 9 May to 22nd I developed German measles, and felt really rather rotten and extremely depressed and weepy. After a few days I had a short note from Terry – very scrawly and obviously written with great effort. From then on each letter showed improvement.

I went back to duty on the 19th. Life was more than hectic.

On Monday 22nd Terry was sent to the Officers' Convalescent Home, Ringwood, and said he was feeling perfectly fit. He wanted me to get two days' leave and go back again to see him – but it was out of the question [at this stage in the pre-D-day period]. I didn't even ask for it. He said there was something he must tell me. Later it was arranged that he should have week-end leave – 2 to 5 June.

Friday 2 June [written later] He arrived on Friday afternoon and rang me up at once. He seemed very cheerful and fit and said he did not even feel tired.

When I arrived home about 1930 (having managed to get away early) he had been taken to hospital. After tea he had what appeared to be a stroke, and could not move his right arm and leg.

I went down with Berenice to the Prince of Wales Hospital, and we were told that a clot of blood from the wound in the artery had shot up to the brain. They hoped it would dissolve of its own accord, but proposed to call the brain specialist for the Services in the South West – Surgeon Captain Lambert Rogers RNVR.

I saw Terry that evening. He was still in his battledress, lying on a bed. He smiled at me – it was rather dreadful with only one side of his face able to move – and gesticulated with his left hand to show that he was able to move it. He yawned continually. . .

Saturday 3 June Next morning I went in on my way to duty. He seemed very much the same. I waited until the surgeon-specialist had seen him. He said it was very serious, and that the cerebral artery having been blocked, the blood had been cut off from a large part of the brain. Collateral circulation might take over, but the mere fact of stopping the blood supply would damage the brain. I felt very pessimistic after hearing this. I went back to the office and Peggy[1] arranged for me to telephone to Lambert Rogers at Barrow Gurney – I felt the hospital were being so slow.

When I went back that afternoon I was told that Lambert Rogers was coming down on Friday and that in the meantime there was nothing that could be done for the present condition: all they could do was to decide whether it would be possible to prevent its recurring.

Terry was very restless and complained of a sore throat. He could swallow only minute quantities of fluid. When I got home at 2330, the hospital rang up to say that Lambert Rogers was coming next morning and asked if I would agree if he suggested an operation.

Sunday 4 June Terry was worse this morning . . . I went to the office and came back at 1100 to see Lambert Rogers. He, and [the local specialist], said that as Terry showed no sign of improvement, the only thing to do was to operate to remove the clot. If he were left alone, he would get worse – a large part of the brain would die – and if there should be

---

1. First Officer P. Ahern, Assistant Signal Officer; later Mrs. Morrissey.

another clot it would be fatal. I felt I must take the chance of the operation.

In the meantime Warick had arrived. He stayed at the hospital while they operated, but I could not face it and went back to work. The hospital rang up before the operation was finished to say that it was all right so far. After it was done, Lambert Rogers rang me up and said that it was successful and that Terry had stood it very well, though of course he was not out of the anaesthetic. I went in on my way home; he was still not out of the anaesthetic. I rang up about quarter past nine; Sister said his condition was critical and could not well be worse, and asked me to spend the night at the hospital. I went back again with Warick and saw Terry for a moment. He looked rather dreadful, with his hair shaved off and his face very white. He was still not conscious, but they said he was coming round from the anaesthetic. . .

Monday 5 June I slept in an empty ward – or rather stayed awake most of the time. Soon after six I was brought a cup of tea, and then Sister came in and said he was worse, especially during the past hour. I went down and saw him . . . For a few moments I felt faint but afterwards found Sister and got her to ask the Resident Surgical Officer to see him again. He told me that Terry's condition was very grave. Sister rang his home and mine. I went back and dressed. Soon after that I was told Warick had arrived. We waited a little and then Sister asked us to go to the ward. Then she said: 'I'm afraid he has just died'. He had never regained consciousness.

We came home then.

Everybody has been very kind. The Signal Officer sent Joy out [by car] to say how sorry they all were. But it doesn't help. I just don't know how to start again. I had looked to Terry for support and comfort for so long; absolutely everything was bound up with him.

I am very glad we were married: we had long enough together to know how wonderful it was. The past year has been the happiest of my life. Every time I saw him I loved him more, and he said the same thing at Tidworth – that we loved each other more and more as time went on. It would have been wonderful to live with him and have children – the only thing I regret is that we had not had a child. . .

In the evening I went to see the Deacons. They are very upset, especially his mother. I feel dazed, and every now and then it hits me again, and I realise something new about it. I wish I had not to go on living.

Tuesday 6 June (*Continued*) D-day. Airborne and sea-borne troops have

2nd Lieutenant Terry Deacon, 1943.

landed in France, this morning. Terry would presumably have been in it. I feel I must go back to duty this evening. It settles my problem for the moment – of how to deal with life – by giving me an excuse for not facing it. I cannot forget his face and his breathing . . . He was not quite twenty-five. He gave me a present on the anniversary of our wedding – a book token, and on it he had written 'One wonderful year'. I am glad we both had that much happiness together. We had a very happy leave at the beginning of April – just before all leave was stopped. We stayed at home and did nothing special, but it was very lovely.

Wednesday 7 June The [funeral] service was at noon. I am glad I went; it was rather harrowing but I felt much better afterwards. It was not the stereotyped service, but apparently the Vicar's own variation. Two of Terry's friends [from the regiment] came down and Mrs. Welby and a few other people. After lunch I went on duty.

   Commander Tours has been extremely kind. He asked me if I wanted a move, or leave – but I don't, especially leave. I wouldn't know what to do with it.

Thursday 8 June I find I can't remember things very well – especially if they happened before the week-end. This evening I found I couldn't remember things said to me by Bodycote[1] this morning. I have very little physical energy.

---

1. First Officer D. Bodycote, in charge of WRNS personnel at ACHQ.

CHAPTER III

Invasion of Normandy

Tuesday 6 June . . .I had intended to go on duty this evening, but in the end I didn't. [The Vicar] came to see me in the evening and spent a long time talking to me.

[Third Officer Moira Charlton (now Mrs. K. Macleod), describes in her journal the final preparations and D-day at Dartmouth, where she was Assistant Confidential Books Officer, HMS *Cicala*, which was the base for Auxiliary Vessels: . . .

'. . .*Friday 25 May.*

'Doran[1] rang me up before 8 to tell me that the flap had come, could I get down early? We were all there about 8.30 a.m. and did not leave till 2.30 the next morning. That was the first day. It continued for ten more. Except for one night when I got off at 10, we worked every night till after midnight, and for that first week until 3 and 3.30 in the morning. It was a spell of glorious weather, wonderful out but suffocatingly hot in the small hours in the little blacked-out upper rooms which were the Confidential Book offices . . . Admiralty couriers came in most days with huge loads of bags which had to be counted and numbered, signed for and re-issued without delay to the ships. Two telephones rang continuously, issues of codes were being rushed out to ships about to sail, officers queued at the door and all down the stairs. We were helped by the kindness, thoughtfulness and good humour of everyone around us, in particular the boys of the 1st Motor Torpedo Boat Flotilla. They were all hanging around waiting, and bore us away from our bedlam to drinks and meals in the mess downstairs, chaffed and cheered us, and even one night in the sweltering small hours, came up and worked with us. Work filled one's life but I wouldn't have missed it for anything. One was always tired, with an ache at the back of the eyes, but proud to find one could carry on with four hours of sleep o'nights. For those few precious hours I slept like a log, though at the height of the rush I even dreamed of CB bags and one night I was convinced someone was calling out for a secret envelope!

---

1. Second Officer D.M. Doran, Confidential Book Officer.

'Audrey[1] drove me the interminable round to Brixham, Torquay, Teignmouth and sometimes Exmouth, [where] I had to deal with the Resident Naval Officers ... We sometimes went for hours without meals and then ate them in odd places – supper of beans on toast on board a Canadian MTB, a snack in a Motor Launch, teas at the Northcliff Hotel at Brixham. Some of the officers had rooms there and Dickie Carson[2] once lent his to Audrey and me to tidy up, and we met two very shocked old ladies as we came out of his door ... !

'At Inver Dart [temporary WRNS quarters], the water was turned off at 6 p.m., so when we got in around 2 a.m. or later there was just a stagnant bath of stone-cold water for washing. Bans were in force: no private telephone calls, no telegrams, no talking to civilians, all naval personnel confined to quarters or places of duty. (The Wren officers shut up over in Dartmouth showed great keenness, volunteering to help in the office and to take 'hand of officer' stuff around, which amused us but helped us out!)

Waters[3] came over every other day, mainly loaded with IMMEDIATES for the Landing Craft (Tank) squadrons ... The nights, like the days, were marvellous. Betty Blake[4] used to walk back with me to bed along that lovely Riversea path smelling of syringa, in the most enchanged moonlight.

'*Sunday 4 June.* Audrey and I drove to Teignmouth, giving John M.[5] a lift as we were to bring back his boat after re-fit ... We were diverted to Brixham to allow a convoy to pass, then out the other way to Churston; otherwise we had a free run. The roads were patrolled by police and security police and there were no traffic jams. Though civilians went nonchalantly on their way on bikes or on foot, all civilian cars were stopped and pretty severely questioned. We had to produce our identity cards and passes every few miles, but we were never refused passage except when the road was cleared for convoys. Torbay was a marvellous sight that Sunday, crammed full of shipping of all kinds, destroyers, corvettes, [mine] sweepers ... We called at the RNO Torquay and on to Brixham, where I carried out involved transactions (speaking on direct orders from the C in C. The Naval Officer in Charge[6], Dartmouth, could not get all round and telephones were insecure). Then round the Canadians [at Brixham] and the Harbour Defence Motor Launches, and a 'tip and run raid' on the

1. Wren Audrey Burles.
2. Not identified.
3. Paymaster-Lieutenant R.C.Waters RNVR, Assistant CB Officer, Auxiliary Vessels CB Office, Plymouth.
4. Chief Petty Officer Wren, in CB office.
5. Lieutenant John Mathias, DSC, RNVR.
6. Vice-Admiral the Hon. A.C. Strutt, CBE.

LCT squadron office. The bulky operation orders from Admiralty were a big headache to us and to everyone else. We dumped a heavy load of them in the LCT office, the Squadron Commander being out, and they duly disappeared. (Some ten days after, when all had arrived in France, we found every envelope and bag unopened in a cupboard in the office). We got in at 5 p.m. pretty weary, to find Waters there again. He bore me away forthwith in his streamlined brake to Brixham, Audrey following behind as best she could. We had a harum-scarum drive, nearly crashing on Kingswear Hill, and were diverted up side lanes through Brixham. We tore along the jetty and Waters retrieved an IMMEDIATE envelope which had gone astray. It should have been delivered at 8 a.m. and contained Sailing Orders for a convoy. He then handed it over to me to find the addressee and rushed back to Plymouth. Audrey and I raced back to Dartmouth, dodging convoys, and I boarded the *Seamew* (our CB boat) and searched the river for a certain LCT and a Lieutenant-Commander called Armstrong[1]. I ran him to ground eventually in the deserted bar of the Raleigh Hotel, standing talking to an army staff officer, and I thankfully gave him my IMMEDIATE. He was a nice man. He said he had had no sleep for two nights and my message killed all hope of rest on the third; he was done in before the show started. We were all so tired, we just looked at each other and laughed! He treated me to a drink, then we shook hands and Armstrong made an odd little speech thanking the women for the part they were playing (but it seems so little). I went back to the office bedlam, and he, I presume, prepared to invade France.

'*Monday 5 June* was the last of the hot glorious days. I was out on the river all the morning in *Seamew*, trying to find LCT's and to give them their Admiralty bags and envelopes . . . The river was crammed with landing-craft, nearly all manned by British officers and crews and full of American troops. Jazz music splintered the ancient sunny silence of the Dart. The men, stripped to the waist, lay in the sun and shouted to us, and sometimes threw us sweets; the officers hailed us and gave us last letters to post. It was moving, rather like a nightmare. We waved to them and felt rather sick at heart.

'Back in the sun and wind to *Cicala* and I bolted a cold lunch in the office; then off again with Audrey to Teignmouth and Torquay, and back to Brixham with operation orders for more LCTs. I was met outside the Squadron Office by the old Duty Lieutenant. He said he thought I was too late but we might just catch them. We tore along the jetty, leapt into a boat

---

1. Probably Lieutenant-Commander C.P. McG. Armstrong.

and sailed round the harbour. My boats had already gone but we were in among the rest as they sailed. One by one the engines roared and they moved out. The little snottie [Midshipman] we had always seen in the Duty Office was on board one and he waved goodbye, and the old Lieutenant stood up in the boat and waved back. It was unforgettable.

'Audrey and I raced back to *Cicala*, too overwhelmed for speech, and went up to the CB Office.

'For nearly a fortnight chaos had reigned – telephones, hurrying feet, people coming and going. Suddenly all was quiet. Doran was sitting still; everyone had nothing to do. We had done all we could – it was beyond us now. The effect of that stillness hit us like a blow.

'Outside the landing craft were still streaming out of the river and they went on passing till about 8 p.m. The Wrens, imprisoned in their Dartmouth quarters ... were waving towels and handkerchiefs, which fluttered for hours. The base staff went off duty at 6. The two flotilla CO's and the Commander came up to the office and talked quietly. We went down to supper and a flatness was everywhere.

'Next day, *Tuesday 6th*, I went twice to Brixham and to Torquay. The roads were empty, the woods free of troops. It was misty, grey and depressing and blowing hard. There were rumours of 'D' being put off for a month ... Next day we heard the invasion of France had begun.'

[This description relates to one limited area: in all 702 warships, ranging from 6 battleships to 360 motor launches and other small craft, plus 25 flotillas (i.e. units of 6) of minesweepers, took part in the invasion – with 4,266 landing ships and landing craft.[1]]

Sunday 11 June We are not very busy, in fact the slackest we have been for months. At lunch time I had a telephone call to say that Gordon Groos had come down with Terry's things from Bulford. I took an hour and a half off and had lunch with him and Tommy, a Canadian. The majority of their unit is in France. For the first time since I have had my present job, I came home by the 6 o'clock bus [instead of duty car, which was provided for people working unusually long hours] and went to church on the way. It was a National Day of Prayer, which I did not know, having been so cut off from everything during the past few days.

Tuesday 13 June Every day I have letters returned that I had written to Terry; I don't think he can have had any from me since he went to Ringwood –

---

1. Edwards.

the delay being principally due to the censorship this end. I am sorry he did not get them. I have had letters from a good many people. It all seems more remote now. I still have not really got down to putting things together again, and have been practically apathetic during the last day or two. Every now and then I realise some particular aspect – but the fact still has not really registered, apart from the initial shock. That is not really true – but it is true to say that I have not got beyond the immediate present.

Saturday 17 June The fighting in Normandy is heavy, and places are changing hands two or three times. But on the whole things seem to be going fairly well.

During the past two nights the Germans have been attacking Southern England with pilotless aircraft, which are presumably radio-controlled. It appears that the plane itself explodes at the end of its journey. [These were of course the notorious V.I's, alias Buzz Bombs.]

Saturday 24 June My darling Terry's birthday. Lois sent me some ... flowers, which I thought was rather sweet. He would have been 25.

Friday 30 June The inquest was held today, having been delayed for the report of findings of the Court of Enquiry into the original PIAT accident.

Cherbourg was captured a day or two ago. There is very heavy fighting still in the Caen sector, where the 6th Airborne Division are fighting and Terry presumably would have been.

'Southern England', which appears to mean London, is being attacked regularly both by day and by night by the pilotless aircraft, or flying bombs as they are now called, after further investigation. They are not radio-controlled, but are apparently set on a course at the time of launching. They are jet-propelled, and the weight of explosive is approximately equal to a 2,000 bomb.

[Petty Officer Wren Phyllis Hansell, then an Officer Cadet, describes some aspects of life at the receiving end:

'When I went to Greenwich for OTC we had to sleep on the ground floor of the Nurses' Home on palliasses, which had to be taken up in the lift to the top floor, where we had our cabins. As this was the time of the Buzz Bomb, life, to say the least, was somewhat disturbed. One morning when we were all in a state of undress, either getting a bath or washing, we heard a very ominous sound and everyone dashed out into the corridor. You have never seen such a funny sight of naked and half-naked Wrens in your life, and once the bomb had crashed we stood and roared with laughter at the sight.

'...We had to take our meals in relays in the Painted Hall so that there were never too many people in there at one time, and if there was an "immediate alert", all the stewards departed to the shelter, and we just sat and ate on so that we could at least get something to eat.

'At the end of the two weeks' course the Buzz Bombs were quite awful and on the Saturday after lunch three of us decided to get a taxi and get away from Greenwich. This we did and the driver took us to town to our three separate stations and refused to take a penny fare from any of us. When I got to Hayling Island [near Portsmouth] I remember going to bed at 9 p.m. in utter peace and sleeping until half-past seven in sheer exhaustion after hardly any sleep for two weeks.'

...We are suffering from an acute shortage of water – a very uncommon thing here – due, I suppose to the large number of US soldiers and sailors imported during the past year, combined with a long drought. During the past few days the water supply has been cut off in the evening, starting an hour earlier each day (today it was 1500), which is very inconvenient. However, I suppose it can't be helped. There has been some heavy rain this week. I took a day off today, but felt rather worse than I do on duty. Everything seems so pointless. Last Thursday was my first day off since I came back from having german measles – not counting the week-end 6 June – and Letitia and I went out to Bedford Bridge and walked down to Grenofen. It was a lovely day and very pleasant by the river watching the dragonflies, birds and trout; but I felt really rather miserable because it all reminded me so much of Terry. We had walked down there more than once, very happy, and the last time he took me out we had tea at the horrible little cafe in Yelverton, as we did today ...Almost every day I have a letter from some one or other: people are very kind, but they persist in thinking it brave of me to go back to duty, whereas it was actually the easiest thing to do. I don't know what I should have done without a job to occupy me. Which doesn't mean that I am particularly pleased with work, but it is better than not having anything definite to do.

Sunday 16 July ...On my last day off I spent practically 30s on gramophone records – a Bach suite played by the Adolph Busch chamber orchestra.

Wednesday 19 July A new offensive has been started at the eastern end of the Normandy front and is going quite well. General Montgomery has recently decorated members of the 6th Airborne division for their part in the fighting in the Caen sector...

London and the Southern counties are still being attacked with flying bombs. The Germans are full of tales about bigger and better ones – the latest of which, according to them, could reach New York.

Letitia's birthday.

In the office we are in the process of reduction from our peak of 71 (47 of them officers). Life is not nearly so hectic as it was before D – in fact I have been rather bored lately. But that may be due to the fact that I have been very depressed and bored with things in general.

There is still no leave except for people living within 30 miles of the port.

Thursday 20 July There has been an attempt on Hitler's life. Hardly anything is known about it, except that it was made by bomb and was unsuccessful. Hitler escaped with burns and bruises, but one or two members of his staff were killed.

I spent a pleasant evening at the WRNS quarters with Joy, Pat and Priscilla, having a crayon portrait done by Valerie[1]. I was rather pleased with it.

Tuesday 25 July News from Germany is still very vague and confusing. According to the Nazis, the plot was made in Russia, the bomb manufactured in England and placed under a portfolio on Hitler's desk by a general. The Chief of General Staff (Seitzel) has been replaced, and Himmler[2] has been put in command of the German army at home. The attempt is said to have been organized by a 'tiny clique' of ambitious generals.

It is very difficult to get any idea of what really is going on, because all news from Germany other than official announcements has been stopped, and the various rumours are vague and contradictory. Some generals have been shot, and according to one report, armed Gestapo men have been patrolling the streets of Berlin. At the same time the Nazis declare that their position is stronger than ever and that loyalty to Hitler has increased. The Nazi salute was yesterday made the Service salute instead of the normal one – which seems to be considered highly important.

The King is on a visit to Italy, having gone by air, and Churchill has returned from a second visit to Normandy.

---

1. Third (later Second) Officer Valerie Moon; afterwards Mrs. D. Macleod.
2. Heinrich Himmler (1900–45); in command of all police forces including the Gestapo, i.e. *Geheime Staatspolizei*, the Nazi secret political police.

I had two days off at the week-end, and spent Saturday night and Sunday with Berenice and a friend of hers in her caravan at Maker. It was quite pleasant, but rather constricted.

Wednesday 26 July Hitler has proclaimed a state of 'total war' in Germany, and has appointed Goering to see that everything and everybody is mobilized for the war effort, and Goebbels to carry it out.

The renewed offensives at each end of the Normandy front have made slow progress against very heavy resistance.

The Germans are still sending flying bombs over London and Southern England. The [launching] sites in the Pas de Calais are attacked from the air frequently and heavily. One of the latest attacks were also directed against a starting-place for rocket bombs, which so far have not been used against this country. . .

Friday 28 July . . .In Normandy there is no news from the British sector, but the Americans have advanced almost to Coutances. . .

Saturday 29 July . . .The weather continues dull, oppressive and damp; work is slack and uninteresting and I am very bored. What I should like to do is to go abroad; everything here is so stale, and I am tired of the foul air [in the underground offices, which in the pre-invasion period had had to accommodate about twice as many staff as the air-conditioning system had been designed for]. It is all very depressing.

Monday 31 July The first sunny day for weeks. I went up to the Pavilion [on the cricket ground at Mount Wise] for lunch, and had it outdoors in the sun with Valerie and Priscilla.

The Americans have taken Avranches, at the south of the Cotentin peninsula.

Tuesday 1 August I have asked to be sent abroad – I can't stand it here now: there is not really enough work. I hope to go to Italy.

Thursday 3 August The Americans have reached Rennes and are advancing fast, without a great deal of opposition.

I am told that my name is at the top of the list for foreign service. There is no vacancy at once [for a First Officer]; in the meantime I am to go to Western Approaches for a short time.

The King has flown back from Italy.

Transfer to Liverpool

Saturday 5 August The signal came today appointing me to *Eaglet* for Western Approaches on the 12th [Everyone was nominally appointed to a ship, even at a shore establishment. There was always some, perhaps very humble, vessel bearing the name.] But I hope to have some leave before I go. This morning I ordered a tin trunk from Austin Reed and a hat box [in the hope of going abroad later].

Had supper with Peggy in her flat.

Sunday 6 August The Americans have cut off the Brest peninsula, having reached the Loire – though it is not certain at what point. Leading tanks have entered Brest.

The third fine hot day – far too good for work.

The past two days have been really busy, in the old way. It is strange to think of going to Western Approaches with no US Navy, no offensive sweeps in the Channel [with] all our daily flaps and panics. [Almost every day there had been a rush to get urgent signals out to destroyers or other vessels designated to carry out operations during the following night. Western Approaches Command had been established, as indicated earlier, at the stage when the prime objective had been to combat the depredations of U-boats among merchant shipping and its work was aligned to the Atlantic rather than to narrower waters.]

Saturday 12 August My leave was finally approved [after some argument with the WRNS head office], thanks to the Signal Officer and the Chief of Staff[1], who made a signal saying I had been sent on leave for reasons of health. I spent this morning saying good-bye to the Superintendent, COS etc. It is not known how long I shall have to stay in Liverpool.

Sunday 13 August I stayed in bed until 1130, had a leisurely bath, did the flowers and spent the rest of the day lying in the sun. It was bliss.

---

1. Commodore (later Rear-Admiral) C. Caslon CBE.

Monday 14 August Joy and I took our lunch on to the moor by Horrabridge, and then met Pat for tea at the Magpie. Very lazy and very pleasant. Joy had to go on duty at 1800, but Pat and I stayed on, finally coming back in a petrol lorry.

Tuesday 15 August There has been a new landing by US – British sea and airborne troops – in the South of France, between Nice and Marseilles. It was made early this morning and is going well. . .

Wednesday 16 August Saw the film, *Pygmalion* for the second time. It is very good.

Thursday 17 August Went to the bank to clear up Terry's account. . .

Friday 18 August The landings in the South of France have now penetrated about ten miles inland. In the North, Orleans has been taken, and Chartres . . . The Russians have reached the East Prussian frontier.

I had lunch in Quarters with Joy and Pat, and stayed on to tea. Collected my old Service hat from being cleaned and re-blocked – 3/6d. It is four years old and still good enough for wet days. My packing is going very slowly. I am still waiting for my tin case. I have not been able to get a hat box, which is a nuisance.

Saturday 19 August This morning I went into ACHQ to return my ration-book and pass, and to get my duty [travel] warrant. Said goodbye to Commander Tours, Peggy, Mac[1] and so on. This afternoon we all went to see Leslie Henson's show, *Africa Stars*. It was really very good, and extremely funny in places – including the inevitable 'Rachmaninov Prelude' act. [This was an exaggeratedly dramatic performance, as it might have been done by an exhibitionistic pianist, but punctuated, as far as I can remember, by various 'technical hitches'.]

The area covered by the landings in Southern France is now a thousand square miles. In the north, patrols are said to be 'probing' the outskirts of Paris, advancing from the region of Dreux. It seems incredible that they can have reached Paris so soon.

Sunday 20 August I went to church this morning. My packing is practically done now, except for the last-minute things. . .

---

1. Second Officer A.N. Macdonald, one of the Duty Signal Officers.

Monday 21 August I travelled up to Liverpool today by the 0845, which arrived at about 1920 – almost an hour late. It was very crowded – up to thirteen people in the compartment and sitting or standing solidly in the corridor. No food obtainable of course – I had some with me – and no room to move. Mostly civilians travelling. I got out at Mossley Hill and was met by two of the cypher officers, who had organized a taxi for me.

Tuesday 22 August Went to Derby House and began to learn my new job [which was the equivalent of the Plymouth one]. I have not seen Commander Edwards (Signal Officer[1]) yet – he is on leave. As a result of my having had leave, I am taking over from Second Officer Williams[2], who has been doing the job since Davidson left. Liverpool is vast and grimy, fully of huge buildings black with soot. Derby House is even more difficult to find one's way about than the Moat, but my job, I think, will be simpler. One of the first people I ran into was Captain Lush.

The quarters I am in (Bruckley House, Mossley Hill) are quite pleasant – an old-fashioned house in a quiet and rather pleasant suburb. I have a room to myself and my own bathroom, and am the senior body there and the president of the mess committee.

Wednesday 23 August Paris has been liberated. It was announced at midday that after four days' fighting in the streets, the French within the city have succeeded in freeing it from the German occupation – after four years and two months. There is no official news of the progress of the American columns beyond Paris, but a report from Algiers says that one has reached the Marne. The British and Canadians are advancing south-east from the region of Caen and the Falaise pocket has been cleared up, resulting in thousands of prisoners. The force landed in the south has taken Grenoble.

Friday 25 August Rumania has agreed to surrender unconditionally to the United Nations and to help fight against Germany … It is thought Bulgaria may take similar action. Paris is apparently not yet completely free. There is still fighting inside the city and American troops are on the way to help the FFI. Southern France is said to be more or less under the control of the French, and the Vichy Government has gone 'somewhere else'.

---

1. Commander K.P.M. Edwards.
2. Second Officer (M.E.?) Williams.

I called on the Superintendent (Carpenter[1]) yesterday morning, but did not have a chance to say my piece about wanting to go overseas.

The shops in Liverpool are marvellous – quite pre-war, with plate-glass windows, lifts and very good supplies, so far as I can judge. [Other parts of the city had, of course, been severely bombed.] I felt quite a fool when I went to have my hair done at Lee's this afternoon – I didn't know how to begin to find my way about. They have some lovely things – carpets and furniture particularly.

I have my suit brushed for me every morning, and a cup of tea brought up by the steward who calls me. There is a naval bus to and fro – and I get away from the office by six, which is luxury. Usually there is time to go out for lunch too. [Life in quarters produced some odd incidents. We were mystified by the strange pale grey colour of the coffee, and its equally strange flavour – till the officer in charge[2] of the group of quarters investigated and found that it was brewed once a week in a bucket and re-heated day after day.]

There are quite a few people here whom I know from Plymouth. Gert Workman[3] looked in today to brush up her cyphering. I have rather more than 48 officers, and 12 ratings. [This provided the cypher office with twelve cypher officers and three rating typists for each of the four watches.]

Saturday 26 August . . .It has been a lovely day – this evening it was hot enough to lie in the sun. We are allowed to wear plain clothes on Saturday and Sunday after 1400.

---

1. This is a mistake: it was Superintendent A.J. Currie CBE.
2. First Officer J.G.G. Mackie.
3. First Officer G.E. Workman.

1945

CHAPTER I

Kyle of Lochalsh

Kyle of Lochalsh, Wester Ross, Scotland
[Before the diary resumes, the War in Europe had ended, on 8 May.]

Sunday 10 June . . .I did not stay in Liverpool very long. I was not well and after a month or two asked to change my job completely. It was not very easy, though Commander Edwards was very kind about it; but in the end I left in mid-November [1944] and went to London for an interview with Chief Officer Nye[1]. It was decided that I should do the [WRNS officers'] Secretarial course at *Demetrius*, starting on December 16 – which gave me three weeks' leave. That (leave) was the one thing I had been longing for – it had been such an effort to carry on. [To make the change possible, I voluntarily reverted to Second Officer.]

Demetrius [the Supply and Secretariat School, at Wetherby, Yorkshire], was pretty grim. The staff were nice and the course not too bad; but the whole set-up was so much like a mild form of concentration camp that it got one down. It wasn't helped by the extreme cold – 31 degrees fahrenheit of frost one morning – which made sitting in classrooms quite painful and walking from block to block anything but pleasant on frozen snow. The course lasted six weeks – two weeks too long, in my opinion; we were all stale by the end of the month.

[It was in fact an interesting and useful course. The title 'Secretarial' is rather misleading, since the subjects covered were mainly administrative and legal.] We were familiarized with KR and AI, AFO's and CAFO's (respectively, Kings's Regulations and Admiralty Instructions, Admiralty Fleet Orders and Confidential Admiralty Fleet Orders. No ordinary work of reference, however complicated, can hold any terrors for anyone who learned to track down specific items in the last two, as then issued.) We were taught to calculate mulcts of pay (a form of punishment), to prepare

---

1. Chief Officer P.D. Nye.

preliminary documents for courts-martial, to write Formal Letters, such as one's Commanding Officer might need to send to his Commander in Chief, for example. These had to be in the stately style beginning, 'Sir, I have the honour. . . ' and ending 'I have the honour to be, Sir, your obedient servant'. We were initiated into the arcane details of Service Certificates – the documents drawn up for every sailor at the beginning of his service. They were of great importance, because they contained every relevant detail – name, description, date of birth, home address, depot – e.g. Portsmouth, Devonport or Chatham – the name of every ship he served in and the relevant dates, his advancement to Leading Seaman or Petty Officer, any punishments he incurred, and an annual assessment of character – Very Good, Good, or Fair – depending not on personal opinion but on the absence or presence of any punishments for offences. This document went with the rating on each new drafting, and he was entitled to see it once a year. In the 1940's the certificates of the older men were still on parchment – or parchment-like paper, with a greasy surface difficult to write on: the newer ones were on linen-reinforced paper, but all of them double foolscap size, folded in half, and of course hand-written. If a sailor deserted, his certificate was marked RUN, and the top right-hand corner cut off. A simplified form of certificate was used for Wrens.]

Demetrius was, of course, organized as a ship, and it must have been there that I first came to grips with the naval system of time-keeping. The day is divided into four-hour watches (except for the two dog watches of two hours each, in the evening). Each half-hour is denoted by a bell struck by a sailor, probably a sentry in the case of a shore establishment. Thus 0830 is one bell in the forenoon watch, 0900 two bells, and so on to 1200 = eight bells, starting again at 1230 with one bell in the afternoon watch.

The instructors were naval officers of the Supply and Secretariat branch, denoted by (S) after their rank. This had superseded the former style of Paymaster – lieutenant, captain or whatever it might be. They were mostly young, and very able – a surprising number of them left-handed. We used to do the *Times* and *Daily Telegraph* crossword puzzles together every day, completing both in the twenty minutes or so between the last morning lecture and the beginning of lunch.

Over Christmas there were the usual rituals of officers waiting on ratings at meals. I have the printed programme of a Ship's Company 'Variety Entertainment' performed on three evenings about that time – but have no recollection of it at all.

We were given a long week-end, in which I went home, arriving [at Plymouth at 0730 on Saturday instead of 2330 on Friday through being delayed by snow] and left on Sunday night for my new job as Secretary to the Naval Officer in Charge, Lochalsh [HMS *Trelawney*], where I arrived on Tuesday evening. The journey was dreadful: cold, and held up by snow for a whole night in the train at Perth. [There was no restaurant car on that train: I lived on an enormous pie my mother had made for me, using a tin of pork originating, I think, from USA as a special import. Occasionally it was possible to rush out with one's mug to a station buffet and get it filled with tea, or even to buy a roll – but that was very much a matter of chance.]

I took over from Lieutenant (S) J.F. Down RNVR as Captain's Secretary, and (to my horror) from Third Officer Rapp[1] as Officer in Charge WRNS and WRNS Quarters. [I also found myself Education Officer and Resettlement Information Officer. These latter involved only occasional activities, but meant that I had to brief myself about the subject matter in order to be prepared for them. Supervising the Quarters was another matter: keeping accounts and mustering the stores and equipment, which seemed mysteriously to change from one muster to the next. Some of the items had strange names. I remember being baffled by something listed as 'knife, prong, one': after wasting a great deal of time, I found that this was an antediluvian form of tin-opener, barely recognizable as such.]

I lived in the Wrennery after the first day or two in the hotel. Having three completely new jobs, for two of which I'd had no training, I found life somewhat strenuous. And at that time there was quite a lot of social life, *Philante* being in most of the time. [This was a large motor yacht, converted into a depot ship for anti-submarine craft, and there were quite a lot of invitations to informal events. There were also the anti-submarine craft themselves – very small ships, whose young officers were very hospitable. A favourite occupation was playing Ludo, of all things, sitting round a minute table in their cramped wardrooms, which seemed to have been designed for dwarfs. At any rate it led to a lot of hilarity. Getting into and out of the vessels was quite a feat in itself. They were lying alongside the quay, so that when the tide was out, the decks were something like eight feet below the level of the stone pier, and one had to climb down a narrow vertical iron ladder, in the dark and often in wind and rain.]

There was one tragedy: a Sea-Otter aircraft attached to *Philante* crashed into the loch one day, killing three officers, including the ship's Surgeon-Lieutenant RNVR (Jack Blyth), who was known and liked by everyone.

---

1. Third Officer L.S. Rapp.

There had to be an enquiry, at which it appeared that the flight was unauthorized.

The Wrennery was understaffed and we were cut off from the laundry at Fort William on account of the weather. What with work and personal chores, I never stopped. It was a very small base and not busy, but there are so few people to do the work it seems more than it is. Even now when there is an Officer in Charge WRNS[1] [who arrived in late May or early June] I find I have plenty to do ... In fact we were a good deal busier after the end of the War than before.

[U-boats which were at sea when the War ended were directed to Loch Eriboll on the north coast of Scotland to be disarmed and then came to us, because we were the nearest railhead, for the crews to be taken off and sent to prisoner-of-war camps. Two or three extra cypher officers were lent to us to cope with the additional signal traffic this generated.

In the evening of VE day all the Wrens disappeared down to the various vessels in harbour to celebrate. It was all very innocent, but one had to get them back to the quarters and that took a little time. Earlier in the evening a very young midshipman knocked at the Wrennery and asked to be directed to the quay. He had obviously drunk more than he could cope with, but his drunkenness took the form of extreme politeness, with many apologies for causing trouble. I was a little concerned about his ability to find his way, but evidently he managed it without falling into the sea, since we heard no more about him.]

When I went down to breakfast one morning, the first of the U-boats was coming up the loch.

...A large party of Wrens, including me, were taken over one of the U-boats on 17 May; and we had one or two good parties and a picnic at Dornie with the officers of the escort group. I had been going on leave on 10 May, but it had to be put off till 4 June on account of the extra work involved.

The Naval Officer in Charge is Captain B.C. Gourlay; and the other officers are Lieutenant-Commander C. Nithsdale, Commander (S) E.F. McNeill Smith, Lieutenant-Commander (S) M.N. Godfrey RNVR, Surgeon Lieutenant Commander P.S. Hawkins RNVR and Third Officer N.M. Petit...

I live in the hotel now, which is very comfortable and modern and very expensive (4 guineas [£4.4s] a week is the reduced Service rate. [The offices were also in the hotel, on the top floor.]

---

1. Second Officer the Hon. Olive Lawson-Johnston, known at her own request as 'LJ'.

Saturday and Sunday afternoons I have free as a rule, but if it is wet, one works, because there is nothing else to do. Usually we go walking [i.e. with some or all of the last three mentioned] either in Skye or to Balmacara on the mainland, unless the weather is quite hopeless. It is usually unsettled, but one doesn't mind that.

We found a heronry at Loch na Bieste [Skye] on Saturday – it always has to be Saturday for Skye, because the ferries don't run on Sunday. That is to say Godfrey, and I, and Commander Saunders (Naval Intelligence Department) [temporarily at the Kyle]. It was rather wonderful, especially as I hadn't seen a heron's nest before. There were three nests, two with half-grown birds and one with a tiny chick and two eggs. The next Saturday Godfrey and I went again, with Doc and the two WRNS officers lent from Greenock; and this time the two eggs had hatched. The bigger birds were still in their nests. It is quite a scramble to get there, and I don't think the others really enjoyed it very much.

I came home on leave on 4 June for fifteen days (9 days' seasonal leave plus 2 for travelling and 2 interim plus two VE). All the Base officers saw me off except of course the Captain and Number One [Lieutenant-Commander Nithsdale]. It is almost a ritual here seeing people off and meeting them. There are only two trains a day – none on Sundays – and practically the whole village turns out for the occasion. It is really quite funny.

[In February I received the following:

Admiralty SW1   17 February 1945

Madam

I am commanded by My Lords Commissioners of the Admiralty to inform you that they have had before them a report of your good services in the planning and execution of the operations for the invasion of Normandy, and I am to say that Their Lordships have noted with satisfaction the part you played in this great enterprise.

I am, Madam,
    Your obedient Servant,
        (signed) H.V. Markham]

Acting First Officer Audrey Dora Deacon WRNS]

CHAPTER II

Goodbye to the Highlands

Tuesday 12 June ...There is to be a General Election next month. There is postal voting for the Services at home and in the nearer commands overseas. Churchill is carrying on in the meantime with a re-constituted Government.

I am finding my leave very dull. The weather is wretched – not a fine day yet and there is nothing of any interest to do. With Joy gone, and Pat (on Sunday last) and Priscilla sick, there is hardly anyone here that I know. I shall be quite glad to go back, in spite of release, resettlement and what not. (Certain categories of men, such as those needed in industry), and high-priority married Wrens, will start to be released next week. It's very unsettling to know that the base is closing; I don't want to go anywhere else in the UK, and I should loathe the Far East. What I would like would be to go to Europe, preferably with Commander Tours' outfit [part of the Control Commission in Germany]. As for knowing what I propose to do after the War – it's impossible. Sometimes I feel I'd like to do some sort of social work and sometimes I prefer the idea of working as secretary to somebody or something. It's very difficult. One thing I do know is that I don't want to stay at home – it would send me crackers. I realise too that after the War the financial situation will be anything but easy, when my father will no longer be serving. They presumably won't be able to keep this house on. I shall have to have a job that produces a reasonable amount of money ...The people I am with are infinitely more pleasant than I am likely to have any connection with after the War. [Fortunately this proved to be quite wrong!] And I cannot pretend that it is nice to be at home: it's so dull and boring. I feel very much ashamed for various reasons – one of the main ones being that I seem to have recovered from Terry's death far more completely than I would have thought possible ... [This was in fact a very superficial impression: it took a great deal longer.]

My religious beliefs are as inchoate as ever ... Last summer I did honestly try to straighten out my mental muddles; but it was no good, and ultimately I have given up even trying to think about it. Since then I might as well have been a turnip.

This afternoon Surgeon-Lieutenant Lockhart[1] came to tea. He was a friend of Jack Blyth, who was killed when Philante's Sea-Otter crashed at Lochalsh some weeks ago and his home is at Portree [Skye].

I become more and more bored with each day of my leave. Faute de mieux, I have played the piano a lot, but I'm getting tired of that now. When I go back to duty, there isn't time to think: I work till 1900 or 1930 and after dinner we talk over our coffee.

General Eisenhower has been given the Freedom of the City of London and the Order of Merit. A good thing for Anglo-US relations, I should think.

Friday 15 June Ribbentrop[2] has been found in a boarding-house in Hamburg. All the German party leaders have now been accounted for: Hitler is believed to have been killed, Goebbels poisoned himself, and Himmler, the latter while in Allied hands. Goering is a prisoner. [Later he poisoned himself.] Mussolini was shot in peculiarly sordid circumstances by Italian patriots after a so-called trial, and his body was hung head downwards in public, with that of Farinacci[3]. [I heard the news of this last in a strange way, while walking along the lochside, from the public address system of a destroyer anchored about a quarter of a mile away – which made it seem even more bizarre and gruesome.]

...Parliament was dissolved today after a life of nine years, six months and odd days – the longest since the Restoration Parliament (18 years).

Sunday 8 July ...I have been back at Kyle since Tuesday 19 June, after a very comfortable journey up. I had a first-class sleeper from Euston to Inverness, which makes a tremendous difference. Monday afternoon I spent in London between trains. It was very hot and tiring but most enjoyable. I travelled by tube and escalator for the first time (usually I go by bus) – from Euston to Oxford Circus. Down Oxford Street to Bumpus, where I bought some bird books, then down Bond Street to Piccadilly. I had tea, and then happened to notice that I was outside the Academy – so I went in and had a very rapid glance round, knowing nothing whatever about any of it – but on the principle of doing anything once. I walked on to Trafalgar Square and back to Euston by bus.

On arrival at Kyle, I was met by Michael Godfrey and LJ – very pleasant. I was glad to be back.

---

1. Surgeon-Lieutenant R.J.J. Lockhart RNVR.
2. Joachim von Ribbentrop (1893–1946); Foreign Minister 1938–45; previously Ambassador in England.
3. Roberto Farinacci (1882–1945) one of the most extreme Fascist leaders.

We have done some interesting things during the past few weeks. One Saturday afternoon we took the Base skiff and rowed over to Kyle-akin, taking a look at Casteal Moil on the way. It poured with rain, and we came back like 'drookit crows', as the hotel waitress put it. Another day LJ organized a large-scale outing to Dunvegan. Almost everyone went . . . I let my two writers go instead of me. That was on a Wednesday. On Friday of that week I went with the Admiralty courier by road to Aultbea, via Achnasheen. Lovely country, especially by Loch Maree, but the courier in question is such a snob and a bore that I find his conversation somewhat trying. [Also I was feeling car-sick]. Had lunch in the mess at Aultbea, which is a bleak bare place, not nearly as nice as Kyle, and were back in time for tea. It was quite tiring, but worth it to see the country.

On Saturday 30 June we took the boat again and got one of the Motor Fishing Vessels attached to the base to tow us over to Loch na Bieste, landing at the foot of Ben na Caillich, which we then proceeded to climb. It is about 2,530 feet and looks easy walking, but isn't. Personally I had had more than enough by the time we'd finished . . . Michael, Doc and I got to the top – and the view was wonderful: down Kyle Rhea to the sea, and out to what was probably South Uist, and mountains by the score to landward. We put a stone each on the cairn, and then came down, which process I found rather more trying than going up. The boat stuck on the beach and we couldn't get it off till the MFV threw us a heaving-line – which I had to wade into the water to get while Michael and Doc pushed. Unfortunately dragging the boat off opened a hole, through which the water came in quite fast. But by baling all the way we managed all right. Unfortunately we were too late for tea – a major tragedy!

Yesterday LJ hired a car, which she drove herself and took us (Michael, Doc and me) to Port na Long, near Carbost [Skye] in an attempt to buy a spinning-wheel. (She is a most extraordinary woman: makes her own gloves, does carpentry, paints, dyes the wool from her own sheep and now wants to spin.) We didn't get one but we had a wonderful drive through Skye – along the coast, past the Cuillins, and over to the western side, where we could once again see one of the Outer Isles, and along the coast towards Dunvegan.

[It was possible to borrow the Base car and driver for recreational purposes, and this we did once or twice, once for a crazy picnic with some of the young officers from one of the small craft, when we cooked weird messes – almost inedible – halfway up a mountain. The seaman driver was a crofter in civil life, and on seeing a bullock caught in a bog on one of the expeditions, he did not wait to ask permission to stop, but pulled up and went to rescue it. Being a Highlander, its horns were straight and one had become embedded in the soft ground, in such a way that it couldn't move its head to get up and would have died. Many of the sailors were Reservists, crofters from Harris and Lewis, drafted to Lochalsh so that it would not be too difficult for them to get home for the special leave which was granted to them so that they could help with the harvest and other seasonal work, including the important job of cutting and carrying peat for winter fuel. There were also a few WRNS ratings from the Outer Isles, who likewise obtained special leave to help with carrying the peat. All the islanders spoke Gaelic and English, and most of them seemed to be called MacLeod, which was confusing at times.

My officer was on the top floor of the hotel, looking out across the loch to Ben na Caillich, which means Hill of the Old Woman, or Witch. One day when it had been snowing, I said something about the weather to the six-foot Stornoway sailor who cleaned the offices. His reply was: 'Ah yes, the old lady's got a white hat this morning.'

There was one English sailor, a real cockney, who became so attached to Lochalsh and the Highlands generally that he was planning to move there with his family after being demobilized. Opportunities for recreation for the sailors were limited, to put it mildly, and inevitably there was a lot of drinking at week-ends. I came to expect a visit from the Police-sergeant every Monday morning, with a gentle complaint on the lines of 'Somebody's thrown a brick through the Co-op. window, Miss.' Occasionally some slightly rowdy attention – but never anything serious – was paid to the WRNS quarters. One evening during my short period in charge of that building, the Wren cook complained that there was a sailor hanging about and making a nuisance of himself. I felt I had to stage a demonstration of some kind to cheer her up and strode out into the darkness saying firmly 'Is anyone there?' and hoping I sounded braver than I felt. Later she found courage to tell me what she 'didn't like to say' at first – namely, that it was a case of indecent exposure. I duly reported it to the Captain and believe that the culprit was traced, though I never heard the result.

There was one court-martial during the time I was there, involving one of the Motor Fishing Vessels, and I had, of course, to prepare the papers for it. I was asked by the WRNS office to interview a Wren who had deserted and was living at the Kyle. At the time members of the WRNS were not subject to the Naval Discipline Act, so there was not much that could be done about desertion. I always thought it was wise, since it was not likely that a recovered deserter would be particularly enthusiastic about her duties. At any rate, I wrote to this girl asking her to come and see me, which she did. She had very good medical reasons for her action, though they would not have qualified her for discharge; and after a very amicable discussion, we agreed that this was so and I reported accordingly to the WRNS authorities. Nothing more was heard.

Preparations for paying-off are going ahead. While I was away, we reduced to Resident Naval Officer status and we have begun de-storing the offices. I shall be very sorry to leave; hope I don't go anywhere else in this country. Naomi [Petit] has gone, and a lot of the Wrens, and a few of the older sailors have been released.

For our last church service we had the usual chaplain (Artus[1]), [who came from Greenwich every few weeks [on the other Sundays the Captain conducted the service] but instead of having it in the [Base] Cinema as usual, we borrowed the Church of Scotland building, which was infinitely nicer. LJ played the organ – a great improvement on the Wrennery piano . . . [LJ remembers this incident, and another: 'Quite recently someone . . . told me that he had read in a book written by Mr. Macpherson (who owned the chemist shop and wrote books about that part of Scotland) that I had played the organ for that final naval service in the Church of Scotland (I used to play for them on Sundays as they had no organist at that time) and that I had asked him if he thought we could have that service in the Church rather than in the base, and he thought that the Minister would not approve of a Church of England Service in his church. So he rang the minister up and . . . without giving him a chance to say 'No', said: 'I know you will agree' and rang off. Mr. Macpherson continued that the Navy paraded through the village to the church and that I presided at the organ!!'

'The Captain asked me to make a flag to present to Miss Moon [the manageress of the hotel in which the offices were accommodated]. It was a foul anchor and a tearful dolphin (do you remember on top of the flag-staff there was a metal dolphin?) appliqué'd on to a large piece of scarlet bunting. On the last day we hauled down the Union Jack and ran up the flag with suitable speeches to Miss Moon and the staff. I visited the hotel several times after the Navy had left and each time the hall-porter produced a colour party and raised the flag in my honour – much to the astonishment of other people staying in the hotel.']

People – i.e. the Wrens and the Medical Officer – are passing round autograph books and generally getting slightly sentimental.

---

1. The Revd. H.N.M. Artus.

Polling-day was 5 July, and in spite of the numerous memos. produced by me on the subject, not very many did vote by post. The results will not be announced till 26 July, to allow for postal votes to be counted. Some constituencies in North-west England are polling on July 19, it having been postponed for them on account of summer holidays (Lancashire wakes weeks etc.)

Monday 9 July Partial eclipse of the sun this afternoon, which was not noticeable here because of heavy cloud and rain. Whether it affected the weather I don't pretend to know, but the afternoon was extraordinarily oppressive and stuffy. Then we had heavy rain; in fact all the ingredients of a thunderstorm other than thunder and lightning.

Tuesday 10 July This morning I had a salmon sent home (3lb, costing eleven shillings). They pack them beautifully, in a sheath of rushes. I only hope it doesn't get stolen on the way. [It didn't, but arrived quite safely.]

Monday 16 July Paying-off day. The day seemed to consist very largely of goodbyes. Yesterday we had the [priority] men for dispersal in to collect their papers. The Captain saw the Chief Petty Officers. I saw them all and tried to say goodbye to all of them, but several of the sailors were too shy. This morning everyone was at the station to see the main body off. They had reels of adhesive tape (used in the signal department) for streamers – all very gay and American-style. I missed the best moment of all, when Chief Petty Officer Booth ('General Booth') kissed No. 1. Doc went off at 0830 in the [steamer] *Loch Mor* to Mallaig; LJ was to go on the 0600 train on Tuesday. BSO [the Base Supply Officer, Commander McNeill-Smith], Michael and I and our ratings are staying on: my office only till next week.

Tuesday 17 July The Captain went off by road this morning. After I had seen him off, I changed into my old suit and a blue shirt to get down to the serious clearing-out of the office. We had already been partly de-stored as far as furniture was concerned, but had hardly made a start on the papers.

It was quite a strenuous week really – physically tiring, which was quite a change for me. Almost every day I had to go down to the incinerator with confidential papers to burn – which meant a lot of standing, and one horse-fly bite, incidentally. However, it didn't give much trouble.

During the week we had instructions that Sylvia Swift, my Wren writer, is to go to Australia, so I let her go on Thursday instead of Monday 23rd. On Wednesday I had her and Jean Drury[1], my Petty Officer writer, to dinner in the hotel. I think they enjoyed it – certainly we had a very good dinner of trout, followed by a wonderful meringue-ice-strawberry concoction ... I forgot to say that LJ and I had dinner with the Captain and the courier on Monday. Quite the most sumptuous meal I've seen since the War – soup, lobster, followed by steak etc. and sweet. One felt quite ashamed.

By the end of the week I was feeling very sad at the prospect of going. On Saturday we (Michael, BSO and I) went to Kyleakin for the last time and had the usual walk, followed by tea at the King's Arms. After we came back, spent some time with Michael wandering round the pier and generally 'looking my last'. I hate to think I shan't be seeing it again.

Sunday 22 July Wet all day. I did no work but got up late, did most of my packing and then took Lieutenant Dunlop[2], Women's Royal Canadian Naval Service (i.e. the equivalent of a Second Officer), who is spending a week-end in the hotel, over the Wrennery and round the camp. This afternoon it was too wet to do anything. Michael and I went to church, and then up the Plock [a local headland], with the rest of the party. It was not raining much, but it was far too misty to see the Cuillins, or anything at all. (LJ gave me a little painting she'd done of the Cuillins, from the road towards Plockton.)

Monday 23 July I left Kyle by the 1135 train, feeling very sorry indeed. Michael and BSO came to see me off, and all the paying-off party was there, because Jean Drury and one of the pay office Wrens on foreign draft were going too. It was raining when I left, but before we reached Dingwall the sun was shining, and going through Perthshire, the mountains were wonderful. I travelled via Perth, and managed both to get dinner there and to catch the 1030 from Paddington [next morning]. No sleeper, but I slept quite a lot.

---

1. Later Third Officer.
2. Her correct title was Lieutenant J.L. Dunlop, Royal Canadian Navy.

CHAPTER III

A Dry-Land Ship

(Plymouth)

Thursday 26 July This morning before I got up a telegram arrived to say that I am to report pm 31st to HMS *Fledging*...

The election results were announced today – Labour has a majority of 152 (I think). Personally I voted Conservative – more because I thought Churchill and Eden were two good men to carry on in their present jobs than for any other reason – but I'm not really surprised that Labour has won. After all, the Conservatives had been in since 1935, and before the War, at least, weren't particularly bright. But nobody was then, really. Of course one can't agree with any one Party completely; they each have their good points and bad. Churchill had come back specially from the Potsdam conference in time to learn the result. The conference (between the 'Big Three' – Churchill, Stalin and Truman) had not ended.

My leave is so short that I seem to be spending it mainly in housework [quite spontaneously, needless to say!] and mending my clothes. However, this afternoon I broke out and took Letitia to a film, *The Picture of Dorian Gray*. It was quite good, though the leading man was as near inanimate as made no difference.

Saturday 28 July Details of the new Government have been announced [including, of course, several members of the war-time Coalition.] Attlee is Prime Minister, of course, Bevin[1] Foreign Secretary, Dalton[2] Chancellor of the Exchequer, Herbert Morrison[3] Lord President of the Council. Attlee and Bevin have gone back to Potsdam (Attlee was there with Churchill.)

Japan is being attacked daily from the air and several times has been bombarded by British and US ships. The 'Big Three' issued a proclamation a day or two ago inviting Japan to surrender; but it was disregarded – naturally, Japan being if anything more suicidally inclined than Germany.

Today I bought Richard Perry's book, *I Went a-Shepherding*, which describes, among other things, his life on a farm near Kyleakin, and seems

---

1. Ernest Bevin (1881–1951); later Lord Privy Seal.
2. Hugh Dalton (1887–1962); Baron (life peerage) 1960.
3. Herbert Stanley Morrison (1888–1965); later Baron Morrison of Lambeth.

to be very interesting, especially in view of my local knowledge. This evening I have been brushing up my King's Regulations etc. for the benefit of *Fledgling* – *Trelawney* didn't give me much experience of the more normal side of Captain's Office work, particularly of disciplinary matters.

Weather isn't too good, but I lay in the sun for a little while this afternoon.

Thursday 31 July Travelled up to *Fledgling* – a fine, hot day. The trains were fairly full, but I had a seat all the way. For a relatively short journey, it seemed to take a very long time – from 1040 till about 2100. A car collected me at the station (Norton Bridge, instead of Standon Bridge – RTO's routing, of course!), but I had to leave my bicycle.

I am taking over from Second Officer Varian[1], who goes to RN Air Station, Crail, on Monday.

Wednesday 1 August. Fledgling is a hutted camp used for the technical training of air mechanics, mostly British, but including a fair number of Dutchmen, who were intended to form the nucleus of the Netherlands Fleet Air Arm in due course. Previously *Fledgling* had been responsible for training Wren air mechanics. The Dutchmen were young and very light-hearted; having a working party of them to clean my office each Saturday morning was to prove a hilarious experience. Conscious of the approach of noon, when they would be off duty, their knowledge of English would suddenly desert them if they were asked to do anything extra, e.g. 'Could you polish my desk, please?' 'Polish? (pronounced like the nationality) Polish? What is Polish?'

My staff consists of one Leading Wren [Adams. She kept a pet rabbit, I discovered later. It used to sleep at her feet, under the bedclothes – no doubt forbidden, or would have been if anyone had envisaged such an eccentricity, but she was never found out.] The certificate work is done by me [see p. 136].

I can't say I'm very pleased with the look of the place. My cabin is a reasonable size, and I share a bathroom with Second Officer Scott[2], the Unit Officer. There is a cold-room outside the window which makes a very tiresome noise most of the day and night; but this, I am told, one gets used to! The wardroom is almost adjacent (under cover) and has a billiard table and a ping-pong table in one of the rooms. The food, of course,

---

1. Second Officer M.A.Varian.
2. Second Officer E.E. Scott.

doesn't compare with Kyle (not that I expected it to, but I don't think it's up to normal naval standard). [At Lochalsh basic things like cabbage were fairly scarce, but things normally regarded as luxuries, such as salmon and lobster, were plentiful, being caught locally.]

Saturday 4 August It is expected that there will be a railway strike (over working conditions) during the week-end.

This afternoon I went 'harvesting' with the Medical Officer[1]. [As far as I can remember this was a scheme under which one offered one's doubtfully valuable services to farmers, in view of the shortage of labour.] It consisted of sitting in a cornfield in the sun watching the cutter and binder – no work at all. Very pleasant – the hot sun is lovely if one isn't in uniform. Lay in the sun after tea too.

The Captain is a very pleasant person – Captain P.R.P. Percival, DSO, RN Retd. He is leaving next month.

One doesn't work here on Sundays – unless one wants to. Breakfast is later than on week-days; then church at 1030 (we have our own padre[2]).

Thunderstorm about lunch time, so my basking plans were frustrated. I am becoming rather more reconciled to the place – but the officers are a very odd lot – some quite nice, others not. The country round about is pleasant but entirely featureless. I'm told one can see the Wrekin (20 miles away) on a clear day. It is farming country, gently undulating, with a lot of trees, little streams and dozens of intersecting lanes which are very pleasant for bicycling. On Friday evening, in the cool after dinner, I got Adams to conduct me on a bicycling trip. We cycled for about an hour and a half, and only had to get off once for a hill.

Further Government appointments have been announced – I think all the ministries are filled now. A. V. Alexander[3] is First Lord of the Admiralty again.

The Potsdam conference is ended. On his way back, President Truman met the King on board the *Renown* at Plymouth the other day.

Wednesday 8 August The main news today is that the first atomic bomb has been dropped, on a Japanese town of about 300,000 inhabitants [Hiroshima]. It has not been possible to see what damage has been done, on account of the thick cloud of dust covering the area; but the force of

---

1. Name not recorded: he was on temporary loan.
2. The Revd. F.T. Horan, RNVR.
3. Albert Victor Alexander (1885–1965); had been FLA under Churchill 1940–45; 1st Baron Alexander of Hillsborough 1963.

the bomb is calculated as 2,000 times that of the 10,000 [high explosive] bomb, which is the largest yet used. The new bomb is based on the power liberated by splitting the atom; and it is said that this source of power will be able to be used for commercial and industrial purposes after further research. The research carried out up to now, by British and US scientists, has been going on throughout the War and has cost £500,000,000. It was not decided to use the new weapon until after Japan had rejected the Potsdam offer of peace.

This evening I went for a walk with Third Officer Green[1] – a very pleasant person – and we stopped at a cottage to buy some sweet peas. The woman who opened the door told us that Russia had declared war on Japan.

Friday 10 August A second atomic bomb has been dropped – on Nagasaki. At 1300 today we heard the first news of Japan's reported offer to surrender, provided that the position of the Emperor will not be affected by so doing. There was, up to 2100, no confirmation from any Allied Government – apart from a Russian announcement that the Russian Ambassador, who had not had time to leave, had been received by the Japanese Government; but the offer has been announced by the Japanese Domei news agency. As usual with these things, it is more than one can truly realize. It takes a little while to change one's whole perspective.

The atomic bomb has made a tremendous sensation. One feels more than ever that another war would mean the end of the human race. Germany was also working on the same theory – but fortunately hadn't got far enough to make use of it on us. It is said that the principle is so well known that all nations will be able to make use of it, and there is talk of control. Churchill, before going out of office, drafted a statement, and President Truman has spoken, about the potentialities for good and evil of the discovery.

Tuesday 14 August Throughout the week-end there were rumours, and denials of rumours, that Japan had surrendered. We listened to every news bulletin; my Wren even brought her wireless to the office so that we shouldn't miss anything. By this evening we were half inclined to think that perhaps they weren't going to surrender after all. However, one had hardly settled down in bed when there were shouts and whistlings and what not: I looked out of my door to see what was happening and was

---

2. (Later Second Officer) E.J. Green.

greeted by a dustbin lid [rolling] along the corridor. The surrender had been announced at midnight by Mr. Attlee. We all got up and went out; the ship's bell was rung – to such an extent that the Dutch fire-party rushed out looking for the fire! We had been preparing a bonfire for VJ day itself, but someone set light to it now, and it began to blaze. It was a wonderful bonfire. There was an effigy of Tojo (or Hirohito?)[1], which was duly burned. The wardroom piano was carried out on to the grass, and we sang songs, English and Dutch, and vaguely rushed round the fire for an hour or so. A barrel of beer was broached and we retired to the wardroom for drinks. Then out to the bonfire again – and then rounding up the Wrens and checking them into the cabins. It was quite a job, and we didn't get back to our beds till about 0330. Fortunately the Captain decided that there was to be Sunday routine today (Wednesday) – I spent a few minutes in the office, and that was all. We had a service, on the lines of the VE service, and then the day was our own. I was very tired and went to bed after lunch – so did almost everybody – and slept quite a long time. In the evening there was an Anglo-Dutch variety show (planned for to-night before we knew it was VJ), which was quite good, [All performers were members of the ship's company.] Followed by a ship's dance, which I thought was pretty grim. Joyce Green, Isobel Linden[2] and I went, and Scottie for a little.

I should have said that we 'spliced the main brace' this evening – my first taste of rum, which I didn't like much. Strictly speaking, WRNS personnel are not entitled – but one doesn't win a war every day. I had only half a tot, and had to disguise that with orange in order to drink it.

I just can't really comprehend that the War is over. Six years is a long time, and all our ideas have been focused one way, so that it's very hard to take in the fact. The Chinese had had eight years of war – it must be even more wonderful for them.

Opening of Parliament this afternoon.

Thursday 16 August Wardroom dance, which I didn't enjoy at all. We were allowed to wear plain clothes, but owing to the suspension of posts over VJ and VJ + 1 – both were public holidays – my long dress didn't arrive and I had to wear an ordinary one. Not that that made any difference. But I don't like parties unless I'm with people I know and like.

Saturday 18 August Went to Newcastle-under-Lyme with Isobel to meet

1. Respectively Prime Minister and Emperor of Japan.
2. Third Officer Linden.

Vicky Erskine[1]. We went on to Hanley, did a little shopping and saw a film.

Sunday 19 August Bicycled to Newcastle with Joyce and had lunch, tea and supper with Vicky. It was very pleasant to get out of *Fledgling*. She is in the WRNS quarters at Clayton, in an old house with a nice garden. I felt rather tired, but better than yesterday.

Monday 20 August The trial of Marshal Pétain, which has been going on for some days past, has ended with his being sentenced to death, which seems very cruel in view of his age (89). Evidence was given by Daladier[2], Reynaud and Laval, who has yet to be tried himself. I think these war-guilt trials are rather futile: one knows pretty well beforehand what the verdict will be – and in any case I don't really see how one can honestly blame people for the co-operation we should have praised if it had been with us instead of the Germans.

Tuesday 21 August The United States has announced the end of Lend-lease – which makes the financial outlook for this country pretty grim. The announcement was made without consulting the British Government; and a Mission is being sent to try and make some arrangement.

...Last week the routine release-signal came for me. I am not volunteering for postponement of release – I think the best thing is to get out and set about finding a job. It is estimated that more than a million men and women will have been released by the end of the year.

This diary is being written a week later – most unsatisfactory, because I miss a lot of details. I must try and catch up; then it will be easy to keep it up to date.

Marshal Pétain's sentence was reduced by General de Gaulle to imprisonment (for life)...

Nothing of interest till Saturday, when Joyce and I went over to Newcastle and Hanley with Vicky again. I did quite a lot of shopping – in order to use my coupons before being released. I bought two petticoat and knicker sets and some knitting wool. Also, as an extravagance, some books – Alun Lewis' last book of verse, Nina Cust's *Not All the Suns*, and two more of the 'Britain in Pictures' series – *British Birds*, and *British Pottery and China*. Had an enormous tea (crumpets) in Hanley.

---

1. Second Officer Victoria Erskine.
2. Edouard Daladier (1884–1970) Prime Minister 1933, 1934 and 1938–40; Prisoner in Germany 1943–45.

Sunday 26 August A warm sunny day, after a lot of grey and showery ones. This afternoon a party of us went off in the 'tilly' [utility van] to Brockton Golf Course, where we watched a match between Padgham, Compston and King. Knowing nothing about either them or the game, I didn't take a very intelligent interest; but it was very pleasant walking about in the sunshine. Afterwards we had a picnic tea on Cannock Chase, and then drove to the Cock Inn near Standon Bridge and drank lager. Back to supper and then over to the Petty Officer Wrens' sitting-room for their gramophone concert, or rather part of it, including the Brandenburg no. 5. After that I got involved in a conversation with the padre . . . on peculation as found among Government contractors etc., and couldn't break away till nearly 2300.

Reading *Tristram Shandy* just now, which I find most entertaining. It's a little hard to remember that Sterne was a parson – one would never guess it from the book!

Among my numerous omissions from this diary is all mention of the various operations of which details have now been released – Mulberry [the pre-fabricated mobile harbour invented for the invasion of Normandy], Pluto [pipe-line under the ocean, for oil fuel] and Fido [something like fog, intensive, dispersal of] and radar. (Radar, of course, being a series of devices rather than an operation). While I was at home on leave I saw the Mulberry exhibition, which was very interesting, with scale models of the various components of the harbours and of the various types of ships and craft.

Tuesday 28 August Yesterday evening a few of us went on a so-called educational jaunt by lorry to Barlaston Hall – not knowing quite what to expect. It is a rather fine old house belonging to the Wedgwood family, now used as a centre for Army non-commissioned officer instructors, who go there for a fortnight on a course in some one subject and then go back to their units and 'spread the light'. The staff instructors are civilians, such as university lecturers on vacation. Lengthy arguments on Lend-lease etc., took place – also supper, a little half-hearted dancing and some ping-pong. Actually it was quite fun.

Today yet another jaunt – this time to Lichfield. Two of the Wrens were to be confirmed there, and the padre took Joyce and me along as passengers. The service was conducted by the Bishop of Stafford, who gave a rather long but interesting address, on the atomic bomb among other things, in the little chapel of the palace. We had a very quick look round the cathedral beforehand. After the service, we walked through the sleepy little town in hot sunshine, bought some pears – great luck – and then had tea and drove back, arriving soon after 6.

Wednesday 29 August Thunderstorms during the night and again this morning, and literally torrential rain for the greater part of the day.

I spoke too soon about Sterne – since then I've had a sermon on conscience, and a moralizing preface!

[It was about this time that I was woken up one night at about 1.30 a.m. to send a signal to the Admiralty, as required by regulations, reporting that one of the young naval ratings had developed diphtheria – provisionally diagnosed by the Chief Petty Officer Sick Berth Attendant. Our own Medical Officer being away, we had to call in the medical officer from a US army camp a few miles away, who confirmed the diagnosis and duly explained the quarantine regulations to the Captain. He was, no doubt, astonished when the latter observed that no one would be able to go ashore, and that he would have to stop the liberty boats. Like any other naval establishment, we were regarded, miles inland though we were, as a ship, and after a time it did not seem at all strange to hear references to decks, galleys, and other such nautical manifestations. The expression 'liberty boat' must go back, I think, to the days when many of the sailors were recruited by the press gang; those who had volunteered, but not the pressed men, had their liberty at certain times when the ship was in harbour, or near enough for them to go ashore by boat. In the case of *Fledgling* it meant that the liberty-men 'going ashore' formed up just inside the main gate and marched out in a body at the appointed time for the 'liberty boat' to get the bus to Hanley or wherever else they were going.]

Saturday 1 September This afternoon I went into Stafford with Scottie, who came back from leave on Thursday. We did some shopping – I bought a blouse, a pair of camiknickers, and – very luckily – the collected poems of Sidney Keyes . . . We had a horrible tea at the Railway Hotel, and then saw a rather pleasant (British) film called *For You Alone*. However, I refuse to believe that (as it showed) Heddle Nash would ever sing the song of that name at a symphony concert accompanied by the London Symphony Orchestra – which had an astounding programme, beginning with the overture to *The Merry Wives of Windsor*, and including a Beethoven symphony, a concerto and about half a dozen other things! Nevertheless we enjoyed the film, particularly for its naturalness in the village scenes and its general unaffectedness.

The Padre is to go to RN Barracks, Chatham, and the Medical Officer to Portsmouth, to the disgust of both of them. The former MO, who has been on unpaid leave as a Parliamentary candidate (unsuccessful), is to come back. . .

Sunday 2 September The Japanese signed the armistice terms today on board USS *Missouri*, in Tokyo Bay.

I was duty officer, which means that I couldn't go out, though it was a lovely day. Played the piano after tea. Like everything else, I don't do it well. I seem to suffer from chronic mental sloppiness nowadays.

Monday 3 September The sixth anniversary of the British declaration of war on Germany. Turning back to look at what I wrote on this day last year, I opened the book at the day of Terry's accident. I can't bear to read it – and yet I had to read part of it – all of it. One thing is still true – that I'm not facing life. I have never yet managed to straighten out my ideas – to work out a basis for living. I don't actively want to die now, and I'm a little past the state of caring whether I live or die – with a slight animal bias in favour of living. But I'm still [dodging] the spiritual problem . . . I had hoped that I had got over my . . . fear of people – but no. Worse than ever in fact – and I am making no effort about it.

Thursday 6 September I am taking my VJ leave (2 days) plus interim (2) and a day for travelling in order to go to Lois (Hoskin)'s wedding on Saturday. Travelled down overnight, arriving at 0600 (almost 12 hours).

Saturday 8 September We went by taxi all the way to Sheviock Church [a few miles into Cornwall] where we arrived too early (naturally)[1]. It was a grey and rather chilly day and at one time seemed likely to turn wet. Lois didn't wear white, but a sort of frock and jacket affair in [gold]. They had an old-fashioned sit-down wedding breakfast, with toasts, speeches etc. – and the number of aunts, uncles, cousins, etc., was nobody's business. . .

Wednesday 12 September Returned to *Fledgling* on Tuesday, to find that a signal had been received announcing the appointment of my relief – one Second Officer Cannell[2], from Dundee. She is to arrive next Monday, and we are to report to D. WRNS the day I leave duty. The date we proposed was Friday 21 September. Whereupon D. WRNS comes back saying that a further signal will be made about my release. (Up to Sunday it hadn't come.) All very unsettling.

1. It was a family failing always to be early for any event.
2. D.M. Cannell.

CHAPTER IV

What Happens Next?

Sunday 16 September I shall be glad to leave *Fledgling*, but quite sorry to leave the WRNS; after six years it is going to be quite difficult to settle down. Also there is the question of getting a job. I would rather like to do some kind of social work, preferably something that entails community life. Something like a settlement or a girls' club – but I don't think I have any particular qualification for the work other than a desire to do it. I shall write to the Appointments Office at Bristol to be registered as one who wants a job.

[About this time Chief Officer Dunlop[1] spent a night or two at *Fledgling*, where she had previously been stationed, on her way north or south for a holiday. As everyone did at that time, we all began to discuss what we would do after release. I described my vague ideas, and found that she had a brother who was Director of the then Tyneside Council of Social Service. She suggested I should consult him, which I did, and after the exchange of a few letters, he suggested that I should approach the Plymouth Council of Social Service. This I did. As a voluntary organization, it had only a small staff, but it happened to have a vacancy for an assistant secretary and offered me the job, thus enabling me to start a new career.]

Yesterday was the fifth anniversary of the culminating day of the Battle of Britain, when 185 German aircraft were shot down.

Tuesday 25 September In what might be described as a lucid interval today, I suddenly and almost unconsciously understood the meaning of integrity – a resolution of internal conflict into one-ness with oneself – and therefore why two opposite classes of people may be called happy: those who have succeeded in absorbing the 'lower' (id) part of the self into the higher (ego), and those who are unconscious of an ego and live without conflict or question. This is presumably obvious and elementary (and somewhat sententious) – but I was quite pleased with my discovery. At least it shows some glimmering of thought after so long without an

---

1. Not traced.

intelligent attitude. For fifteen months I have lived absolutely without any aim or purpose: and for most of that time in a blind unthinking state of numbness mentally. Spiritually I have just not existed.

I wish I could get away from this place. Lately I have been very depressed and bored beyond words. Mentally more stagnant than ever. The work is dull, and not enough to make me feel busy – without which feeling I seem to be incapable of decent work.

Saturday 29 September This afternoon the Captain drove his wife, 2/0 Scott and me to Dovedale, on the borders of Derbyshire, a very pretty place rather in the manner of Double Waters but not as good. But it was very pleasant, and good to see hills again. We went at 1500, took a picnic tea and got back about 1900.

I have had a cold this week, but didn't go sick. The first cold for more than a year. . .

Sunday 30 September Harvest Festival. The Captain takes the service now that the Padre's gone. This afternoon Joyce and I bicycled to Sugnall – quite a pleasant ride.

Monday 1 October Still struggling with a flood of monthly, quarterly, half-yearly, etc., returns. Depressed this evening. I thought I was getting over my lack of memory, but today was pretty bad. The stupid mistakes I make are quite incredible.

There was a serious railway accident yesterday – at least 32 people killed, and more than a hundred hurt. It was the train from Perth (the one I used to catch, at 2020), which was derailed near Watford.

The trial of William Joyce resulted in the death sentence, it having been proved that though he was not a British subject, he was a person owing allegiance to the Crown (he had a British passport) and could therefore legitimately be charged with treason. Which I suppose is sound reasoning – but I have a feeling that if he were being tried by a foreign court, we would be rather rude about legal quibbles, etc. He has given notice of appeal.

No verdicts have yet been pronounced on the guards, etc., ex-Belsen [the concentration camp] but I shall be rather surprised if there are any acquittals. They are defended by British (military) counsel, which they chose in preference to German ones. Which seems sane, seeing that it is an Allied court (in fact British, I think). . .

Tuesday 2 October This afternoon I went with an 'educational' party of officers and ratings to the Wedgwood factory at Barlaston. We were conducted round the works and shown all the processes in the manufacture and decoration of earthenware and in the decoration of china. The latter is still made at the old factory at Etruria (Hanley).

The works at Barlaston are the most modern pottery factory in the world: no bottle-shaped kilns — all the firing is done by electricity. 800 people are employed there; and the plans (still uncompleted) include a village, playing-fields etc., for the work-people. The factory itself is on one level and is lighted almost entirely by daylight.

We started at the beginning, where the flint, china stone, china clay and ball clay are received in the unprepared state. These substances are the ingredients of earthenware: for china the mixture is 50 per cent. calcined bone. We saw them mixed, sifted, pressed (into a substance looking like rubber and dry to the touch) and de-aerated until soft and pliable. Then we were shown plates being thrown on the mould — 144 an hour — relief decoration being prepared — and best of all, the 'throwing'. The potter, or thrower, was making great bowls at his wheel, scraping them as they took shape after the first sensual moulding and kneading by hand, and measuring with rule and callipers as they reached the final stages. Near him was a young boy in the first few months of his seven years' apprenticeship, making tiny bowls. The man had the most fulfilled expression of anyone we saw, including the decorators.

The process of transfer-making from the steel engravings was interesting. Two men were doing this while girls nearby printed the designs on to the unbaked clay. Plates were made by men, cups by women (24 dozen a day) — except for those with feet, which were turned by men. Utility cups were 'handled' [fitted with handles] by machine (a Wedgwood patent) but the better ones were done by women 'handlers'. Colouring of both under-glaze and over-glaze designs was done by women, and the burnishing of gold decoration (with tools of agate or bloodstone) and free-hand painting. Stippling decoration was done by a man.

We were each given a little ash-tray in the biscuit state, decorated with the grape-vine relief we had seen prepared and applied by the women and girls earlier on.

Wednesday 3 October . . .My relief has been appointed — 2/0 Mills[1], who is

---

1. Second Officer B.M. Mills

to arrive on the 12th, from the office of Commodore, RN Barracks, Lee on Solent. She'll find this place somewhat different!

Sunday 7 October My departure has now been postponed till the beginning of next month. The Commodore at Lee made a signal insisting on 14 days' turnover in 'this key appointment', and that Mills should have her overdue seasonal leave before coming here (the latter quite a sound idea, but the former fantastic!) She will report here on 31 October, which means that I should get away during the first week of November.

Yesterday I saw the film *Henry V* in Hanley, and enjoyed it very much. It was a joy to hear fine language well spoken again – and the costumes and general decor were delightful. Laurence Olivier directed the film as well as playing Henry.

I bought a fob watch second-hand for £5.10s at a stall in Newcastle Market. At the time I thought I was a fool, and later, when the watch stopped, I was sure of it! However, it has gone today, though not accurately.

We reverted today to Greenwich Mean Time, for the first time since the War began. As I write this, at ten minutes past six, it is growing dark.

I had a letter from Gordon Groos last week. After having been at Bulford all this time, he is now off to Palestine, where I think it is more than likely there will be trouble over the perpetually vexed question of Jewish immigration.

The trial of Laval in Paris continues. At one time he himself was put out of the court for interrupting the proceedings, which then continued without him or his counsel. (I should have thought this both unfair and illegal – but I wouldn't pretend to know the rules of French procedure.) However, he was admitted to later sessions and seems to have behaved himself. He made allegations that the court was not competent to try him, and that the trial was being rushed for political reasons. Judging from the furore these assertions produced, I should think there might be quite a lot of truth in them.

Yesterday and today have been fine and mild, though fresh morning and evening. Birds were singing (I could neither see nor tell what they were) this evening as if it were still summer. I hear barn owls shriek every night when it is fine and still, but haven't seen one yet.

I am duty officer today – always a trial on Saturday or Sunday. Nothing happens on Sunday: breakfast up to 9.30, then church (I being on duty, had to inspect a church parade of 9 Wrens) conducted by the Captain. I usually go down to the office after the usual 'cupper', but there is not much to do.

Lunch at 1300, then washing clothes, writing letters, darning etc. In the evening the gramophone concert, which this week I am running. The records are provided by ENSA [This organization provided entertainment of all kinds, often involving appearances of famous artistes, to the Services all over the world] and on the average make quite a good two-hour programme. Being DO involves checking-in and 'piping-down' the Wrens [seeing that they had gone to bed], assisted by the duty Petty Officer Wren – which means one doesn't leave their living-block till about 2315 – a bore.

I am reading Trevelyan's *Social History of England*, which is most interesting.

Wednesday 10 October The arrangements for my relief have been cancelled again, for the third time. It is most annoying; not that it really makes any difference to me when I leave the WRNS, but I should like to be able to make some kind of plan. I have obtained from the Appointments Office at Bristol the form of application for enrolment on their register. Some time I shall have to have an interview: on the way south from here would be the most convenient.

Thursday 11 October This place gets duller and duller. I was duty officer; almost everyone else had gone to the Anglo-Polish Ballet in Hanley. I have seen them several times so I didn't much mind missing this once. But the evenings here are almost more depressing than the days. I did some of my knitting . . . while we listened to Tommy Handley – *It's That Man Again* – programme, which had become a national institution during the War. Then I cleaned my civilian shoes and am now writing this – spinning out the time until checking the Wrens in. This afternoon I got my Defence Medal ribbon – but don't know whether I shall wear it.

Laval has been sentenced to death, and has said that he will not appeal. However, his counsel are appealing on his behalf. The whole trial seems to be quite farcical. If it was to be such a travesty of justice, it would have been better not to have had it at all.

The Belsen trial is still proceeding; and also Quisling[1] is being tried, and Hess, as war criminals. It will take some time to work through the list of Germans due for trial, and it seems somewhat futile, I think. But what isn't?

About 40,000 dockers (more than 50 percent. of the total) are now on

---

1. Vidkun Quisling (1887–1945); leader of the Norwegian Fascist party from 1933; aided Nazi invasion 1940; made premier by Hitler 1942.

strike for higher wages in various parts of the country – against the advice of their unions . . . in some places troops are being used to unload the more perishable commodities.

Old age pensions are to be increased next year. There is to be no control of the selling price of houses, the reason given (in Parliament) being the shortage of valuers. Budget Day is to be 23 October. All this is from today's sitting of the House of Commons. . .

Friday 12 October I found a very fine tortoiseshell butterfly in the bathroom this evening, and managed to get him out of the window in my hands unhurt. There are a lot of them about still on fine days: they seem to be very fond of the red dahlias in front of my office.

Saturday 13 October Took my watch back to the stall at Newcastle today. Much to my surprise, they offered to have it cleaned. I went with Vicky, Marjorie[1] and M's sister to see the film, *I Live in Grosvenor Square*, which was good but harrowing. About an Airborne officer and a US sergeant and a duke's daughter – somewhat improbable but very well done.

Sunday 14 October A mild calm day – perfect autumn weather. I took myself out this afternoon and bicycled to High Offley and a little beyond – about 18 miles altogether. It was so mild that I took off my jacket and wasn't at all cold in a thin, short-sleeved jersey. I had been feeling very uncharitable, but seemed to get it out of my system in the fresh air. The country really looked quite beautiful, with a very slight haze softening the sunlight and growing thicker towards evening, when it became quite cold. Scottie has been in sick bay since yesterday, and Joyce goes off on leave to-morrow.

Monday 15 October Laval was shot this morning, after he had tried to poison himself. The appeal was quashed – as one naturally expected. The one o'clock news spoke of people cheering when they heard the shots fired. The whole thing is sordid and corrupt to a degree; even the French Press is disgusted and accuses the court of having made the law ridiculous in the eyes of the world.

The dock strike continues.

Wednesday 17 October . . .Some of the dockers are returning to work.

---

1. Third Officer M. Coates.

The amount of work I do seems to get less each day – which I find most depressing as well as boring. I do hope I don't have to stay here much longer. A signal arrived later this evening appointing a 3/0 May[1] as my relief – to arrive on the 29th. She is coming straight from *Demetrius*, so I feel a little more hopeful about the prospect of her arriving.

Saturday 20 October My 28th birthday.

I went over to Newcastle and Hanley as usual for a 'flick', shopping and tea, and dinner at the Wrennery with Marjorie Coates. For some reason I felt extremely tired by the end of the day. Joyce and Scottie are both away, but it had been arranged with the Captain that I could go out. [Normally there should always have been a Wren Officer on duty.] When I got back, I heard that the ambulance had been lost in Liverpool, where it had gone to take a sailor to Seaforth Hospital, with a Chief Petty Officer driving and two VAD's as passengers. They were all stranded in Liverpool for the night. Apparently there is a lot of car-stealing in Liverpool just now; they left the ambulance in a parking place for about two hours, and when they came back it had disappeared. [As far as I know it was never recovered, and some sort of explanation of this most unlikely event must have had to be given to the Admiralty.]

Sunday 29 March 1946 I left *Fledgling* at the beginning of November and came home for my 56 days' leave, which seemed far too long. . .

On 31 December I started work with the Plymouth Council of Social Service.

_____

2. B.E. May.

Postscript

The appointment with the Plymouth Council of Social Service led to a succession of worth-while and absorbing jobs with voluntary organizations in that field of work. After a year's experience there, I was appointed Secretary of the newly-formed Exeter Council of Social Service. Three years later, in 1950, I left for Bristol, becoming Assistant to the Regional Officer of the National Council of Social Service (now National Council for Voluntary Organizations). This entailed frequent driving to various places throughout the south-western counties, dealing with a wide range of subjects, from old people's welfare to parish councils and village hall committees. In 1962 this was followed by appointment as Liaison Officer for the National Council, in the Eastern Region – based on London and travelling through the Eastern counties north of it, as far as Norfolk in one direction and Buckinghamshire in the other.

When the Hertfordshire Council of Social Service (now Hertfordshire Community Development Agency) was established in 1965/66, I became its General Secretary and Honorary Secretary of the County Association of Parish (now Local) Councils. After being appointed MBE in 1978, I retired in October 1980.

Looking back, I realize how much I learned during the six years of war: without that experience I could not have tackled the responsibilities that came my way later. I am grateful for that, and for some treasured friendships begun in those difficult days, which brought people close to each other in a way that would have taken far longer in normal circumstances. But when all is said and done, it was a terrible and tragic time, and we must hope that future generations will not have to face such an ordeal – which in modern terms would be unimaginably worse – and that the world may at last learn to live 'in the virtue of that life and power that takes away the occasion of all wars'.

References

	Full title
Edwards	*Operation Neptune* – Commander Kenneth Edwards NR (Collins, 1946).
Stuart Mason	*The Wrens, 1917–77* – Ursula Stuart Mason (Educational Explorers, 1977).
Twyford	*It Came to our Door* – H.P. Twyford (Underhill (Plymouth) Ltd., 1945).

Index